Warren Upham

The Geology of Central and Western Minnesota

A Preliminary Report

Warren Upham

The Geology of Central and Western Minnesota
A Preliminary Report

ISBN/EAN: 9783744662055

Printed in Europe, USA, Canada, Australia, Japan

Cover: Foto ©ninafisch / pixelio.de

More available books at **www.hansebooks.com**

THE GEOLOGY

OF

CENTRAL AND WESTERN

MINNESOTA.

A PRELIMINARY REPORT.

BY

WARREN UPHAM,

ASSISTANT ON THE GEOLOGICAL AND NATURAL HISTORY SURVEY OF THE
STATE, UNDER THE DIRECTION OF

PROF. N. H. WINCHELL,

Of the State University.

[From the General Report of Progress for the Year 1879.]

ST. PAUL:
THE PIONEER PRESS CO
1880

PRELIMINARY REPORT

ON THE

GEOLOGY OF CENTRAL AND WESTERN MINNESOTA.

BY WARREN UPHAM.

The area here to be described was explored during the summer and autumn of 1879. It lies on the west side of the Mississippi river, and has this stream for its border 30 miles along the north-east side of Wright county. At Clearwater, 60 miles north-west from Saint Paul, the north-east boundary of this area leaves the river and runs west 50 miles, to the south-east corner of Pope county; whence it extends 120 miles due north, to the north-east corner of Becker county, five miles south-west from Itasca lake. The northern limit of this exploration is a line drawn from the last point 78 miles west, to the Red River of the North, which it strikes 19 miles north from Moorhead and Fargo. On the west the boundary is that of Minnesota for 130 miles, following up Red and Bois des Sioux rivers and along Traverse and Big Stone lakes. On the south-west it is the Minnesota river in its south-east course from Big Stone lake to its northward bend at Mankato, 140 miles; this limit, however, being crossed so far as to include both sides of the trough-like valley in which this river flows. Thence the border is at the east side of Le Sueur, Scott, Carver, and Wright counties; reaching 75 miles from south to north. The extreme length of this area is 250 miles, this being parallel with the upper part of the Minnesota river, its south-west boundary; while its average width is about 65 miles. It thus embraces approximately 16,000 square miles, or one-fifth of the State.

In their order from north-west to south-east, the twenty-two counties included in the field of this report, are as follows: Clay, Wilkin, Traverse, Becker, Otter Tail, and Grant, principally drained by the Red river; Big Stone, Swift, Chippewa, Renville, Nicollet, Sibley, Carver, and Scott, bordering Minnesota river; with Stevens, Douglas, Pope, and Kandiyohi, also drained in large part into this river; and Meeker, McLeod, and Wright, drained principally by the Crow river, which joins the Mississippi at Dayton. The exploration of the topography and geology of this large tract within a single year has been made possible by the similarity of contour and the great extent and depth of its drift deposits, and by the very narrow limits

4

within which the underlying ancient rocks are exposed. These exposures
have been found, with one exception, only along the bottom of the valley of
Minnesota river, and in the valleys of a few of its tributaries, near their
mouths, where channels 100 to 200 feet deep have been excavated in the
drift.

TOPOGRAPHY.

The greater part, probably three-fourths, of this area has a *moderately
undulating surface*, which lies in broad swells of various extent, height and
direction, some of them prolonged, but generally without any uniformity in
trend, while others are oval or nearly round. The highest portions of
adjoining undulations vary from a few rods to a half mile or more apart;
and their elevation is sometimes 5 to 15 feet, again 20 to 30, or even 40 feet
or more, above the depressions, to which the descent is usually by very
gentle slopes. These hollows have a contour that is like that of the swells
inverted, being mostly wide, and either in long and often crooked courses,
of unequal depth, variously branched and connected one with another, or
in basins from one to one hundred acres in extent, which have no outlet but
are surrounded by land 5 feet or perhaps 10, 20, or 30 feet higher upon all
sides. The small swamps which fill these depressions are called *sloughs* or
marshes, the former name being most in use upon the prairies. Many other
depressions, which differ from the foregoing only in their greater depth or
area, contain bodies of water, which vary from a few hundred feet to five or
ten miles in length. All these are called *lakes;* and the term *pond*, which
would be applied to these in the north-eastern United States, is here
restricted to reservoirs made by dams.

Glacial Origin of Superficial Deposits and Contour. The portions of the
earth upon which natural lakes abound are further characterized by surface
deposits of clay, sand, gravel, and boulders, mixed together in the same
mass, which is called till, boulder-clay, hardpan, or unmodified drift. The
rock-fragments are of very diverse material and origin, having been gathered
from ledges that are in place in widely separated districts. The direction
in which these boulders and pebbles have been carried is from north to
south, or to the south-east or south-west, throughout the northern United
States and in adjoining British territory. In these and all other drift-covered
regions the bed-rocks are marked by parallel scratches and furrows, called
striæ, that run in the direction in which the boulders have been transported.
The glaciers of the Alps and of Greenland show us such markings and
similar deposits of drift now in process of formation; and there are no
other known agencies capable of producing these effects. It is therefore a
necessary conclusion that the last period in the geological history of this
region brought a very cold climate in which a vast ice-sheet was accumulated, each year adding something to its depth by the excess of snowfall over
what could be removed by melting and evaporation. Its greatest thickness
was far at the north, where the solid ice probably became several miles
deep; and the pressure of this vast weight caused it to flow slowly outward
in all directions from its deepest part. The superficial materials formed by
decomposition of the rocks before this glacial period, were then ploughed
up, mingled with large additions by erosion of the underlying ledges, and
carried forward in the direction of the ice-current. It appears, also, by
shells and trees found deeply buried between glacial deposits, that this very

cold period was not one unbroken reign of ice, but that this retreated and reädvanced, or was possibly at some times nearly all melted and then accumulated anew. Thus periods of ice alternated with interglacial epochs, in which animal and vegetable life spread again northward, following close upon the retreat of the ice-fields. By each new advance of the glacial sheet much of the previous surface would be ploughed up and redeposited; hence we find only few and scanty remnants of fossiliferous beds in the glacial drift. At the disappearance of the last ice-sheet these drifted materials, seldom modified by water in their deposition, formed a mantle 100 to 200 feet thick, which throughout the region here described completely covered the solid rocks.

The gently undulating contour of most of this region appears to mark areas over which the ice-sheet moved in a continuous current, and from which it disappeared by melting that was extended at the same time over a wide field. The inequalities of surface are very slight in comparison with the thickness of the drift, and the average height generally rises or falls imperceptibly, its slope being often not more than 50 or 100 feet in as many miles. These general changes in altitude, which affect the whole country and give direction to its drainage, are doubtless produced by differences in height of the bed-rock upon which the drift lies as a sheet, probably somewhat uniform in depth; but the small elevations and depressions appear to be due to the accumulation of different amounts of till in and beneath adjoining portions of the moving ice-sheet. This unequal deposition of the drift has produced the multitude of lakes which dot the map of Minnesota. The lapse of time since the ice-age has been insufficient for rains and streams to fill these basins with sediment, or to cut outlets low enough to drain them; though in many instances we can see such changes slowly going forward.

Terminal Moraine of the Ice-Sheet.—The most noticeable deposits of an alpine glacier are its terminal moraine, or the heaps of rock-fragments and detritus which it carries forward to its termination. This frontal line often remains at nearly the same place through many years or centuries. The flowing ice continues to this limit, where it is melted, and the materials which have fallen upon its surface from bordering cliffs, or which it has ploughed up from below, are here left at its end in heaps, ridges and hillocks, of very irregular contour, due to slight retreats and advances of the ice-front, and of greater amount than the deposits which appear upon the area over which it moved, exposed when any climatal change causes the glacier to retreat a considerable distance. Within the field here reported we find similar but much greater accumulations of drift which appear to have been amassed where our last ice-sheet had its termination through a long period. The only notable hills of this area are of this origin. They have no exposures of solid rock, but form part of a belt of rough and hilly drift, where steep slopes and abruptly curving and broken outlines prevail.

This series of hills and rough land extends the whole length of this area, 250 miles; and beyond these limits it appears to be of the same age with a similar belt of hilly drift which has been traced across Wisconsin in the recent geological survey of that state, where it is called the Kettle Moraine. Farther east it is probably represented by similar deposits which cross northeastern Illinois, thence bend north-eastward into southern Michigan, again turn to the south and east through Indiana and Ohio, appear in eastern Pennsylvania and northern New Jersey, and have been traced by the writer of this along the north shore of eastern Long Island, through southern Rhode Island, in the Elizabeth islands, and along Cape Cod to its east shore. West of Minnesota our series of hills is continuous, by a loop that reaches into northern Iowa, to the great drift-range which has been called in its south-east portion the Coteau des Prairies and farther north-west the Coteau de Missouri, extending to the North Saskatchewan river, 350 miles west of Lake Winnipeg. These morainic accumulations, traced more than half way across the continent, are thought to mark the line to which the ice-sheet advanced and where it had its termination through the principal part of the last glacial epoch. At a previous period it reached much farther south, carrying its drift somewhat beyond the Missouri river and nearly to the Ohio. The limit of the ice in this earlier epoch was 300 miles south of our terminal moraine.

Medial Moraines. Before describing these hills in Minnesota, it is needful to mention that other lines of detritus and boulders, called medial moraines, are formed by alpine glaciers wherever they meet from confluent valleys, thence flowing onward together. Series of drift-hills of like origin are associated with the terminal moraine of the continental ice-sheet, which is found to have its course in long curves, convex toward the south and joined with each other by angles that point northward. The glacial sheet is thus known to have had its front divided in vast lobes, each of which had a diverging current, directed at all sides perpendicularly toward its curved frontal moraine. North from the angle of adjoining ice-lobes their currents pushed against each other, and along this line of confluent ice-fields medial moraines were accumulated, consisting of irregular hills, ridges and mounds of drift, of the same character with those that were formed along the margin of the ice-sheet.

The moraine in western Minnesota is partly medial and partly terminal. Beginning beyond the northern limit of our exploration, its course is from the vicinity of Rice lake, near the head of the Wild Rice river, south-south-west 20 miles to the east side of White Earth lake. This portion of the moraine has hills 50 to 100 feet high seen from the top of the new school-building at the White Earth Indian Agency. About this agency the country is prominently undulating, or rolling, having its crests 30 to 40 feet above the lakes which abound. Its general height is about 1600 feet above sea, and this continues to the sources of the Mississippi, 30 miles east. In the next four miles west from White Earth the land descends about 300 feet, to an extensive undulating plain, which has its east boundary at a line running nearly due south 20 miles to the Northern Pacific railroad two miles east of Audubon. Westward this expanse, declining from 1300 to 1200 feet above sea, extends in view from the agency 25 miles, beyond which it again descends 300 feet in three or four miles to the broad lacustrine plain bordering the Red river. The course of the moraine, marked by many small hills of very irregular and broken contour, is due south for its first 30 miles from White Earth lake, passing through the townships of range 40 in Becker county. This belt is crossed by the road from White Earth to Leach lake, which is described as very rough and hilly to the headwaters of Otter Tail river, beyond which it is gently undulating for 50 miles eastward. In the western two-thirds of Erie and Burlington (139 and 138 of range 40) these hills are finely developed ; they rise 50 to 100 feet above the very numerous and irregular depressions, but the general height of the country has fallen off, so that their tops are only 1450 to 1500 feet above sea. Detroit mountain, at the north-east corner of sec. 31, Erie, is one of the highest of these hills. It lies at the west side of their principal belt, which is crossed by the roads from Detroit to Frazee City. On the north road the typical morainic contour is well seen in secs. 7, 8 and 9, Burlington. The coarse unmodified glacial drift, or till, of which our moraine for 250 miles is everywhere made, so far as observed, is here disposed in a great profusion of knolls, short ridges and hills, 20 to 50 feet high.

In Otter Tail county this morainic series continues from the north-west corner of Hobart (t. 137, r. 40,) south-south-west to Spirit lake and Lake Lida, 12 miles. It here varies from one to three miles in width. Its knolls along most of this distance rise only 25 to 50 feet, but they are much more abundant and have steeper and more broken slopes than upon adjoining areas to the east or west. At the south-east side of Lake Lida it forms a range of hills, 100 feet or more above the lake. These are conspicuously seen from the township of Maine, 10 miles south-east. From Lake Lida this moraine widens and covers the first six or seven miles east from the Pelican river, above which it rises 100 to 150 feet or more; being well exhibited for 18 miles in the east portions of Erhard's Grove, Elizabeth, and Fergus Falls. On the road from Maine to Elizabeth its hills are very numerous and irregular in outlines, short, trending from north to south more frequently than in other directions, and separated by hollows 25 to 50 feet deep. Here and for six miles southward, the contour along the Red river and about Wall lake, though within this morainic belt, has been more smoothed than its other portions, probably by floods produced at the withdrawal of the ice-sheet. At Lake Lida these hills have their tops about 1425 feet above sea ; thence to the vicinity of Fergus Falls this altitude gradually diminishes to 1300, not because the hills grow smaller, but because the land on which they lie slopes in this direction.

The region west of this moraine, including the south-west corner of Becker county, the south-east part of Clay county, and the west range of townships in Otter Tail county, extending from the Northern Pacific railroad 45 miles south, and as far westward as to the lacustrine basin of the Red River valley, is mainly hilly, with the highest elevations 50 to 100 feet above the hollows. In the east part of Park (t. 138, r. 44,) and perhaps at some other localities, these hills have a typically morainic contour, being plentiful and irregular, small and steep ; but generally they are massive and broadly rounded, with long gently curving slopes. Indian hill, in sec. 9, Oscar (t. 134, r. 44,) affords a fine view of part of this area and of the moraine seven miles eastward, while at the west it overlooks the plain of Wilkin county, which stretches with very slight descent 20 miles to the Red river. On the east side of the moraine the only prominent outlying hills are at the south-east corner of Hobart, where a gravelly ridge of irregular contour reaches two or three miles from north to south, its highest portion being about 150 feet above the surrounding country. These are the hills which one sees from Perham, looking north-west.

The greatest development of the moraine within the limits of Minnesota, is in southern Otter Tail county, where it sweeps in a semicircle from Fergus Falls south-east to the south line of the county and thence east and north-east to East Leaf lake, a distance of 50 miles. In the first 20 miles, or from Fergus Falls to the north side of Lake Christina, at the north-west corner of Douglas county, it is divided into two or three belts of roughly hilly land, with intervening areas of smoother contour. At one to two miles east from Fergus Falls is a narrow belt of irregular hills and hollows, with the crests about 100 feet above the river. This series continues one to three miles wide for 15 miles south-south-east, through Dane Prairie and Tumuli, into the north-east corner of Pomme de Terre township. Next it partly bends east to the high hills north of Pelican lake, and is partly represented by the less irregular but yet prominently hilly land which lies between Pelican and Pomme de Terre lakes and continues thence a few miles farther south. In Dane Prairie and Tumuli this moraine lies at the east side of a series of lakes, of which Swan and Ten Mile lakes are the largest. Beside the latter, in secs. 27 and 34, Tumuli, the contour for a width of one-eighth to one-fourth mile is in very irregular short hills, 25 to 40 feet above the lake. Their trend, north-west to south-east, is parallel with the lake and with the course of the moraine. These small hills are exceedingly rocky with granitic and gneissic boulders of all sizes up to five or six feet in diameter, which frequently cover half of the ground for several rods distance. North-east from this typically morainic line the land for a few miles is in massive hills and swells, which rise 50 to 75 feet above intervening hollows and lakes. Its least hilly portion is St. Olaf township, which has mostly a rolling surface, in extensive swells 30 to 50 feet high. The east part of Tordenskjold is oc-cupied by a second belt of very irregular hills, which is connected through secs. 19 and 20 and the north part of secs. 7 and 8 with the series that lies at the east side of Wall lake and the Red river, reaching north-west to the broad area of this moraine in Friberg and Elizabeth. The Tordenskjold hills are also joined from the north by another line of drift deposits, having a very rough contour in knolls, ridges and hillocks, 25 to 75 feet high, which extends ten miles with an average width of one mile, from sec. 15, Maine, south-south-east by the east side of Turtle lake. The wide moraine result-ing from the union of these subordinate series continues south-east to Lake Christina. Where it is crossed by the road from Clitherall to St. Olaf, its first and highest hill is called "Dutch Bluff." At the south side of this, about 125 feet lower, is a pretty lake, half a mile long, bordered all around by morainic hills. This belt of short ridges, knolls, and hollows, has a width of three miles thence to the south-west.

The Leaf Hills. In Eagle Lake township, at the north side of Lake Chris-tina, the last described series and that which comes from the south-west by the north side of Pelican lake, are united; and thence for the next 20 miles to the east and north-east the moraine forms a range five to three miles wide, composed of very irregular, roughly outlined hills, 100 to 300 feet high. This portion of the moraine is widely known by the name *Leaf mountains.* We also occasionally hear this name applied to its similar but less promi-nent portions in the west part of this county; and at White Earth agency I was informed that these hills in Becker county are sometimes called a branch of the Leaf mountains. Northeast of East Leaf lake, where the moraine is crossed by the road from Wadena to Otter Tail lake, its elevations rise only about 100 feet and are named *Leaf hills;* which seems a more appropriate title, and will be used in this report to include the highest part of the range. The common name has currency because they are the only hills in this part of Minnesota which are conspicuously seen at any great distance.

Heights of the Leaf hills and adjoining region are as follows: average elevation of south-eastern Otter Tail county, 1375 to 1400 feet above sea; Wadena, 1358; New York Mills, 1418; Perham, 1375; Alexandria, 1391; Evansville, 1354; Lake Christina, about 1200; St. Olaf, 1344; Turtle lake, 1331; Otter Tail and Rush lakes, about 1325; East and West Leaf lakes, about 1340; East and West Battle lakes, about 1338; Clitherall lake, 1341; Nidaros plain, south-east of last, 1450 to 1460; Dutch bluff, about 1450; Leaf hills in Eagle Lake township, 1400 to 1500; in the north-east corner of Lund and north-west edge of Millerville, Douglas county, 1500 to 1600; in Leaf Mountain township, 1550 to 1650; in the north-west part of Effiington, 1600 to 1700; highest summit of the Leaf hills, thought to be in sec. 32, t. 132, r. 38, about 1750; thence for seven miles north-eastward, 1650 to 1600; depression in range crossed by head of Leaf river, about 1425; hills in next six miles north, to where the series is again crossed by this river below East Leaf lake, 1640 to 1450.

The road from Alexandria to Clitherall crosses this range in the township of Leaf Mountain. The summit of the road is near the south line of this township, about 1525 feet above sea. The top of a hill a quarter of a mile east of this and about 125 feet higher, affords a fine view of these "mountains," which westward and north-eastward rise in most tumultuous confusion 150 to 250 feet or more above the intervening depressions They are massive, though very irregular in contour, with steep slopes. No prevailing trend is noticeable. Between them are enclosed frequent lakes, which vary from a few rods to a mile in length, and one of the largest lies at the north-east foot of our hill. The material is unmodified drift, nearly like that which forms very extensive gently undulating tracts elsewhere. The principal difference is that rock-fragments, large and small, are generally more numerous upon these hills, and occasionally they occur in great abundance.

The Leaf hills are also crossed by the road that runs north-west from Parker's Prairie. In t. 132. r. 38, this road winds three or four miles among their knolls, hills and short ridges, rising about 100 feet above the land on each side. Again, in going from Otter Tail lake to Wadena, this range is encountered one to two miles north-east from East Leaf lake. Here its hillocks are only 40 to 60 feet above the hollows, and 100 to 125 feet above the lake. Their material is gravel and sand with enclosed boulders, unlike the stony and gravelly clay which makes up most of these morainic accumulations. This belt of irregular hillocks and hollows, occupying a width of about two miles, next extends in a course a little west of north 12 miles, running midway between New York Mills and Rush lake, and ends (so far as we are able to report) in hills which rise 100 feet above the general level at the south side of Pine lake.

Outlying hills west of this series occur along the south side of the Leaf lakes, where they are 50 to 75 feet high; and for two miles south from East Battle lake, above which they rise about 150 feet. On the east side of this moraine two lines of hilly and irregular contour have been noted branching off from it. The most northern starts four miles south from the east end of East Leaf lake, and extends nearly due east through Inman and Oak Valley into the north-west township of Todd county. On the road from Wadena to Parker's Prairie this line is represented by a nearly level tract of unmodified boulder-clay, in contrast with all the rest of this road which has only stratified gravel and sand. Two miles farther east, in sec. 9, t. 133, r. 35, it rises in conspicuous hills fully 100 feet above the general level. The other series starts from the highest part of the Leaf hills, 15 miles south of Leaf lakes, and passes south-east into Douglas county. In its first few miles this range decreases in height from 200 to 75 feet. At the north line of Douglas county it divides into two divergent belts, both showing a rough and broken surface, though the hills of each are only 75 feet or less in height. One of these continues south-east and east through Spruce Hill township, beyond which it has not been traced; the other runs south-south-west to the north-west side of Lake Miltona, along the west side of Lake Ida, by Elk lake and the west part of Lake Lobster, to the conspicuous hills, about 150 feet high, at the south-west corner of Moe. Each of these belts averages about one mile wide. The latter, in its farther extent, seems to lead by a continuous course from the prominent Leaf hills to the almost equally noteworthy development of this moraine through 40 miles' distance in southern Pope and northern Kandiyohi counties.

It may be here remarked that the Leaf Hills are thought by the writer to be a terminal moraine accumulated at the north-west end of a narrow area, which was not covered by ice in this epoch, but was bordered on its north-east and south-west sides by vast lobes of the ice-sheet. This seems to be indicated by the position of angles in the moraine, with branches, which were probably medial, extending from them; as also by associated deposits of stratified drift which cover extensive areas eastward; while it is obvious that such form of the ice-sheet would correspond to that which it had at an earlier period when it reached farther and surrounded a large driftless area in front of this at the south-east. The terminal moraine formed at the ice-margin in our last glacial epoch is therefore thought to be represented by some branch extending east and south-east from the Leaf hills. That region has not yet been explored in reference to its drift formations; but it is believed that a morainic belt will be found traceable continuously to the drift-hills of Manomin, the south-west part of Ramsey county, and West Saint Paul, there crossing the Mississippi river twice and thence bending east to Lake St. Croix, beyond which its course for the next 50 miles is north-eastward as traced by Prof. Chamberlin, in the geological survey of Wisconsin.

The portion of the moraine reaching from northern Becker county to Fergus Falls or perhaps to the south line of Otter Tail county, and also that from the highest part of the Leaf hills to Pine lake, are then probably medial deposits of drift heaped where opposing ice-currents met. The terminal moraine formed at the west side of the area that is supposed not to have been covered by ice at this time, may be represented by the line of irregular low hills which runs by Lake Ida; but it seems more likely that it is found in the rolling tract, nowhere very rough and broken in outlines but rising in smooth swelling hills 50 to 75 or 100 feet high, extending from the higher hills at the south-west corner of Moe north-westward to Pelican lake and Lake Christina.

From the hills in Moe and the north-east part of Solum, lying on the north and west sides of Lake Oscar, the terminal moraine, seldom much elevated above the adjacent country, but distinguished by its irregular hills and hollows, continues with an average width of about one mile, first south-west and south 12 miles to the bridge across Chippewa river in sec. 32, Nora; then south-east, east, and east-north-east 18 miles, passing along the north side of Lake Whipple to Glenwood.

The height of Lake Whipple (also called White Bear lake) is estimated to be about 1100 feet above sea. It is situated near the center of Pope county, and is the largest lake of the county, being seven miles long with an average width of two miles. At its north side, within a half mile or so back from its shore, the very irregular bluffs of this moraine rise 150, and in a few places 200 feet. This ascent forms the margin of a gently undulating plateau which extends indefinitely northward, with an average elevation about the same as the top of these bluffs. At Glenwood the moraine bends southward around the east end of the lake, and thence it appears to be represented by prominent hills along the line between Barsness and Chippewa Falls, joining the well-marked morainic range of southern Pope county at a point 10 miles south of Glenwood. The broken bluffs bordering Lake Whipple at the north and east are thus regarded as the terminal deposits of ice which was pushed north-eastward, covering the place now occupied by this lake; but before the close of this epoch, the ice-front here retreated several miles, after which it halted, perhaps with some readvance, forming a more conspicuous terminal moraine in Blue Mounds and Barsness, which continues thence finely developed for 40 miles to the east-south-east and east.

The township of Blue Mounds has its name from the hills of this moraine, which begins a mile north-east from the east end of Lake Emily, and extends in a range of very irregular contour, 150 to 200 feet high, or about 1250 to 1300 feet above sea, east along the south side of Signalnas creek, east-south-east through Barsness, by the north side of Woodpecker lake, and between Scandinavia lake and Chippewa Falls, and thence south-east to the south side of Lake Johanna township, where it enters Kandiyohi county. The road from the west end of Lake Whipple to Benson first crosses massively hilly land, 150 feet high, then descends about 100 feet to Signalnas creek, and next climbs about 125 feet among the picturesque ridges and hillocks of the moraine, reaching a point only 30 or 40 feet below its highest summits, which lie within one and a half miles eastward. The range here consists mainly of steep ridges of variable height and length, sometimes a half mile long, running from west to east, with many enclosed irregular hollows. The road from Glenwood to Benson also passes over high swells north of this moraine, whose short, prominent west-to-east ridges it crosses in secs. 20 and 29, Barsness. A beautiful little lake is seen here in a deep hollow of these hills below the road at its west side. Upon reaching the top of the moraine by these roads, one unexpectedly discovers yet higher land within a few miles at the south and south-west, where the north part of Langhei consists wholly of massive swells and hills, 50 to 75 feet above the enclosed depressions and lakelets. This is the highest land in Pope county, being fully 100 feet above the moraine, or 1400 feet above sea. The view from it southward and westward overlooks a gently undulating, but in the distance apparently level tract, 300 to 350 feet lower, extending to the horizon.

The western and southern part of Chippewa Falls gradually becomes more and more hilly as we approach the morainic series at the south and west sides of this township. From Pope Summit, a quarter of a mile north of the village and about 125 feet above the dam, the north-west to south-east range of the terminal moraine is seen rising to about equal height two miles farther south. At the south-west side of Lake Johanna a prominent mass of highland rises 125 feet or so above this lake. Its south-west margin, in sec. 30, descends in rough and broken morainic outlines, forming a part of this series. Here and in its farther course through Kandiyohi county, its highest points are about 1250 or 1300 feet above sea, being 75 to 100 feet above the general level. In the north part of Norway Lake and south-west part of Colfax, it forms a roughly hilly belt two to three miles wide. It is finely seen at the north side of Norway lake and Lake Andrew, where it is called the "Blue hills," or sometimes a "branch of the Rocky Mountains." Its highest knob, called Mount Tom (at south-east corner of sec. 35, Colfax,) commands a fine view. The material of this hill is coarse drift, holding occasional angular boulders up to four feet in diameter and many smaller fragments, mixed also with a large proportion of water-worn gravel. At one point 40 rods north-north-east, boulders up to six feet in diameter are very abundant. The contour here is typically morainic, in short west-to-east ridges of unequal height, very steep, especially on the south side, with correspondingly irregular hollows. Eastward this moraine forms prominent hills in the north-east part of New London and north part of Irving. These cover an area about three miles wide north of Green lake, above which they rise 100 to 150 feet. One of these hills in the south part of sec. 31, Roseville, is called "Sugarloaf Peak." At the south-east corner of Roseville this moraine is called "Cape Bad Luck." The road here climbs 100 feet over a profusion of knolls and hillocks of every form, with no prevailing trend, 25 to 50 feet high above the numerous hollows, which often hold little marshes or lakelets.

This moraine is very prominent from Blue Mounds to Cape Bad Luck, along a south-east and east course of 40 miles. Though it is well known that generally the drift was transported southward, or in some direction between south-east and south-west, it seems necessary to attribute the formation of this range to a glacial current flowing north-east. It appears to mark the north-east boundary of a vast lobe of the ice-sheet, which extended from the Leaf hills to northern Iowa and had its west side at the Coteau. The moraines of its margin were pushed forward by the diverging currents of this ice-lobe, which in approaching its edge were everywhere turned perpendicularly, or nearly so, towards its terminal line. The evidences which usually show in what direction the ice-currents moved, namely, striæ, and the parent ledges from which boulders have been derived, are wanting here, and cannot be appealed to in support of this opinion. No exposures of the underlying rocks have been found in all this region, excepting at one spot seen by Owen on the Red river, a little above Fergus Falls, and commonly along the deeply excavated valley of the Minnesota river, 40 miles south-west. The position of this valley coincides approximately with the axis of this ice-lobe, being so far removed from each of its sides that theoretically it should show no deviation from the axial current. Its striæ, observed at numerous places, all bear nearly south-east. In the absence of these usual proofs, the reasons for our belief are the continuity of this moraine from the Leaf hills to the Coteau by a great southward loop, of which the range of drift-hills in Pope and Kandiyohi counties forms a part; the wide nearly level area of glacial drift, which is enclosed by this looped hilly belt; the occurrence of a medial moraine on the south side of the terminal in Kandiyohi county; and areas of modified drift north of this terminal moraine, sloping away from it, and thus showing that the waters discharged from the ice-sheet flowed in this direction.

The medial moraine alluded to extends from Mt. Tom four miles south-south-east; it then bends south-westward in sec. 30, New London, and is finely seen for 12 miles, passing along the north-west side of Ringo, Nevada and other lakes, to Ostlund's hill in sec. 22, Mamre. Its contour is typically uneven, being composed of a mixed variety of hillocks and short ridges with many hollows. Throughout most of its course its elevation is only 50 to 75 feet above the general level. Its highest points are the two Dovre hills, about 125 feet above adjoining lakes. The road at the south-west corner of sec. 16, Dovre, runs between these hills, which, though of little height, are yet prominent as compared with the rest of this district, so that they are conspicuously seen for several miles around. They are made of nearly the same kind of drift as Mt. Tom, but have more numerous rock-fragments, both large and small. Wherever a prevailing trend is noticeable, it is parallel, or nearly so, with the course of the series, as has been also noted respecting the terminal moraine at several places

South-eastern Pope county contains several areas of modified drift, within two or three miles north of the terminal moraine, which appear to have been deposited by floods from a melting and retreating ice-sheet. One of these areas of stratified gravel and sand forms an elevated plain a mile across at the south-east side of Lake Johanna. It is bordered on all sides by land 50 to 80 feet lower, and its southern portion is about 90 feet above the lake. It has a descending slope to the north, amounting to ten feet in its mile of extent. Another plateau of similar material, extent, height, and slope of ten feet per mile to the north, occurs on the west side of Lake Johanna; and a little farther north, in sec. 6, Lake Johanna, and sec. 1, Gilchrist, are others somewhat lower, also sloping northward. These plateaus of modified drift have steep sides and nearly or quite flat tops. The intervening tracts are gently undulating lowland, also mostly modified drift, 50 to 75 feet below these high plains. The origin of these deposits seems to have been from glacial melting, which washed away a portion of the drift material that was held in the ice-sheet, and spread it upon these areas while they were still bordered on the east and west by ice-walls. The slope proves that these waters flowed northward. As these beds lie in front of the terminal moraine, it appears that they are of slightly earlier formation, or that they belong to some time in this epoch when the ice-front advanced a few miles beyond its ordinary limits.

Another noteworthy area of modified drift occurs in Roseville, north of Cape Bad Luck. Here the terminal moraine is bordered at its north side for four miles by a flat of gravel and sand, extending from two to three miles wide to Crow River, in which distance it descends about 40 feet. This deposit was probably formed by floods, which were poured down from the ice-sheet at the same time that its terminal moraine was being accumulated.

At lower stages of these waters, as in winter, channels were cut in this plain one of these, containing a narrow lakelet, occurs close east of the school-house in sec. 22. Similar, but more extensive plains of modified drift are marked features in the topography of Long Island, Martha's Vineyard, Nantucket and Cape Cod, where they lie in front (which is there south) of terminal moraines, sloping away from them and crossed by old water-courses.

The continuation of the moraine beyond Kandiyohi county forms a wider belt of drift-hills, which seldom have the peculiarly rough and broken contour seen farther north-west. It runs through Meeker, Wright, eastern Carver and south-western Hennepin counties. On the opposite side of Minnesota river it bends south, including the north-west corner of Dakota county, the east half of Scott, western Rice and the east edge of Le Sueur county. These hills rise 40 to 100 feet, rarely more, above the intervening depressions, marshes and lakes. They are massive, with moderately steep or gentle slopes, sometimes being nearly a mile long and properly called swells because of their smoothed flowing outlines. It is also to be noted that the boundary of these morainic accumulations becomes somewhat indefinite; there is a gradual change from the slightly undulating areas at each side to rolling land, and then to hills; and these, usually with no prevailing trend, are scattered more or less thickly upon a belt 5 to 15 or even 25 miles wide. This hilly tract extends through the north edge of Meeker county, by the south side of Koronis or Cedar lake, through the north part of Manannah, and eastward includes nearly all of Forest Prairie township, Forest City, except its south-west portion, and Kingston. Farther south, much of this county is specially hilly and must be reckoned as part of this morainic belt. Of this character are Dassel and the wooded eastern portion of Darwin, Collinwood in less degree, Ellsworth in its north and west portions, Greenleaf, the north-east part of Cedar Mills, northern Danielson, south-western Litchfield and most of Acton. Hills also occur one mile north of Litchfield, and five to eight miles north-west in the wooded portion of Harvey. The same hilly land reaches also north-westward, lying at the south side of the typical moraine, and occupying through Kandiyohi and north-eastern Swift counties a width that decreases from 20 to about 5 miles. The Langhei hills, south of Blue Mounds, are the west end of this tract. These too are its only portion that rises into greater prominence than the terminal moraine. Elsewhere these hills are only 40 to 60, or occasionally, as about Swift Falls, 75 to 125 feet high. At their south-west side the land becomes gently undulating or sometimes flat, as in Lake Lillian and Cosmos, forming the margin of the monotonous expanse of nearly level unmodified glacial drift, which reaches thence 75 miles to the hilly Coteau.

In Wright county it is the shorter task to enumerate the districts which are comparatively level. Such are the east portions of South Side and French lake; south-western Corinna; Clearwater prairie, three miles long; Sanborn's or Moody's prairie and adjacent portions of Silver Creek township; and Monticello and West prairies, together six miles long and two to three miles wide. These areas, like the level tract, nine miles wide, which includes the greater part of Darwin and Litchfield in Meeker county, consist of modified drift, or beds of gravel, sand, and clay, gathered from the ice-sheet and deposited by the waters of its melting. In southern Wright county, the vicinity of Waverly, Howard Lake and Smith Lake, and most of the townships south of the railroad, excepting Franklin in which Delano is situated, consist of nearly level or gently undulating areas of unmodified drift. The swells and hills of this county are mostly 40 to 75 feet high. In its south-east portion they rise 100 to 125 feet above Crow river. Among these hills are numerous lakes, which lie in gently sloping hollows, seldom having steep shores. The most rough and typically morainic area observed is in the south-east part of Silver Creek township, where from Silver lake to Lake Ida the contour is a multidude of small hillocks and ridges of unmodified drift, 30 to 50 feet above the hollows, with no parallelism or prevailing trend. Thence a somewhat similar formation continues five miles north to the river-road. Especially prominent hills, two miles south of Clearwater, and two miles south-east of Monticello, also deserve mention. These hills in Meeker and Wright counties vary in height, descending eastward with the general slope of the country, from 1225 to 1000 feet above sea.

Hennepin county is crossed by this belt of hills in its west and south-west portions, and they are finely exhibited about Minnetonka lake (922 feet in altitude,) above which they rise 50 to 100 feet. In Carver county the townships of Chanhassen and Laketown, the north-west part of Chaska, and northern Dahlgren, are a portion of the same belt of massive hills, with no uniformity of trends, elevated 40 to 75 feet above the hollows. A rolling surface, with swells half as high as the foregoing, continues west to Young America. The remainder of Carver county, excepting its border along the Minnesota river, is gently undulating or nearly level. All these areas are unmodified drift.

In Eden Prairie and Bloomington the moraine extends along the north side of Minnesota river, to within about eight miles south-west of Fort Snelling. The river-bluff here is 140 feet high, and at a mile or two northward these morainic hills rise 100 feet higher, their tops being 950 feet approximately above sea. South-east of the Minnesota river drift-hills, some of which attain equal or greater height, occupy Burnsville, excepting the river valley, and the west part of Lakeville, in the north-west edge of Dakota county. They also cover eastern Scott county to a meridian line drawn through Shakopee. Here these swells and hills generally rise 30 to 60 feet above the hollows, and in some districts 75 to 100 feet. They are most numerous and prominent along a south-south-west course from Burnsville to the south part of Cedar Lake township. Farther west in Scott county, the contour is moderately undulating in swells 10 to 30 feet high.

The western part of Rice county, notably its west range of townships, consists mainly of these terminal drift-deposits, often roughly hilly. In Le Sueur county they give a rolling contour to the east side of Lanesburg, to Montgomery and Kilkenny, and in less degree to Lexington, Cordova, and Elysian; while in Waterville, at the south-east corner of this county, they form hills 50 to 125 feet high south of lakes Tetonka and Sakata. This was the south-eastern limit of my exploration. The continuance of this moraine to the Coteau de Missouri has been already stated. As part of the field-work of next year, we hope to make a thorough examination of that region; and also of that lying eastward from the Leaf hills and thence south to the hills of Manomin, in which distance there seem to be reasons for believing that another terminal moraine, contemporaneous and continuous with the Leaf hills, will be found, marking the south-west limit of a lobe of the ice-sheet that pushed outward from Lake Superior and its bordering high lands. A map of this formation will be presented in our final report.

River Systems. The drainage of the portion of Minnesota here described is not much influenced by the presence of this moraine. Its accumulations rise to great prominence only in the Leaf hills. Generally they are not more than 100 feet high, and are separated by frequent hollows, which allow a free passage to streams. In comparison with the wider areas of gently undulating land, this hilly belt is narrow; and its highest elevations are small in comparison with the greater changes of altitude which come in gradually and almost imperceptibly in traveling 100 or 200 miles, such as that which makes Douglas, Otter Tail, and Becker counties 500 to 700 feet above Minneapolis and Saint Paul. The course of the moraine coincides nearly with the watershed dividing the basin of the upper Mississippi from that of the Minnesota river; but this height of land and consequent division of drainage are probably due to the height of the underlying rocks rather than to the thickness of drift there.

The principal tributaries to the Mississippi river, flowing partly or mainly from this area, are the Crow Wing river, whose branches, Shell, Leaf, and Long Prairie rivers, drain the east portion of Becker, Otter Tail, and Douglas counties; the Sauk river, which has its headwaters in Osakis lake, and in the north-east corner of Pope county; the Clearwater river, draining north eastern Meeker and north-western Wright counties; and the Crow river, which has its waters from the east edge of Pope, eastern Kandiyohi, north-eastern Renville, Meeker, Wright, McLeod, and northwestern Carver counties. The farthest source of the Crow river, in Grove Lake, Pope county, is 90 miles from its mouth, in a direct line.

Winnipeg lake and Hudson bay receive the drainage from the north-west part of our area, by the Red River of the North, which this report, following the example of Owen, calls by this name from the mouth of Otter Tail lake. This is 42 miles east of its junction with the Bois des Sioux river at Breckenridge, where the Red river turns its course ninety degrees, thence flowing north. The Bois des Sioux, a much smaller stream, having its source in Lake Traverse, is the continuation of the nearly straight course of the Red river below this junction. The name Otter Tail river is restricted to the stream which flows to the south 50 miles from the north side of Becker county, passing through Elbow, Many Point, Height of Land, Pine, and Rush lakes, besides others of less size, and emptying into Otter Tail lake. The principal tributaries of the Red river from this area are the Wild Rice river, one of whose sources is White Earth lake, while its south branch drains north-western Becker and north-eastern Clay counties; the Buffalo river, which drains the rest of Clay county, and has its farthest sources near the center of Becker and in north-eastern Wilkin county, and the Pelican river, which joins the Red river from the north 22 miles east of Breckenridge. The last, 45 miles long, in straight line, receives the waters of many lakes, of which the largest are Detroit, Cormorant, Pelican, Lizzie, and Lida. At Fergus Falls the Red river has a descent of about 85 feet, affording very valuable water-power. The Rabbit river is a small tributary to the Bois des Sioux in southern Wilkin county; and the Mustinka river, draining western Grant, north-western Stevens, and most of Traverse county, enters Traverse lake eight miles from its outlet.

The Minnesota river receives only two large tributaries from its north side, namely, the Pomme de Terre and Chippewa rivers. The farthest sources of the former are lakes in Tordenskjold and Dane Prairie, Otter Tail county. Its course is south 75 miles, joining the Minnesota river 20 miles below Big Stone Lake. The Chippewa river, nearly parallel with this and lying 5 to 15 miles farther east, drains western Douglas, nearly all of Pope, the eastern two-thirds of Swift, and the west half of Chippewa county. The other branches of the Minnesota river within this area are small, none of them exceeding 30 miles in length, as Hawk creek, 21 miles below the Chippewa; Beaver creek, again 21 miles south-east from the last; Rush river, in southern Sibley county; Carver creek, at Carver; and, on the opposite side of the Minnesota, Le Sueur and Sand creeks, and Credit river, in Le Sueur and Scott counties.

The watersheds are mostly portions of wide gently undulating areas, interspersed with frequent lakes and sloughs, and have nothing except their slightly greater elevations to distinguish them from the basins which they divide. The erosion of the drift-sheet by drainage has been small in the north and north-east portions of this region, where the valleys, as of Pelican river, the upper part of the Red river, and the Crow river, are not generally bordered by bluffs between which the streams have excavated a passage, or by bottom-lands that have become filled with their sediment. Instead they meander among the hills and swells of the drift, often flowing through lakes, and only having occasional bluffs and alluvial lands along the lower part of their course.

Lake Agassiz. The lacustrine basin of the Red River valley, and the deeply excavated channel which holds Traverse and Big Stone lakes and the Minnesota river, present quite different and more interesting features, produced by the obstruction of drainage in its present course, while the ice-sheet, subdued by a more temperate climate, was yielding its ground between north-western Minnesota and Hudson bay. During this retreat of the ice, great quantities of water were supplied by its melting, loaded, as the modified drift shows, with a large amount of gravel, sand and clay. Wherever there was free drainage away from the ice-front, these materials were deposited in the valleys along which these floods descended toward the ocean. The high water of the rivers, like that which now occurs for a few days in the freshets of spring, was thus maintained through the entire summer; and this was repeated yearly till the glacial sheet had retreated beyond their lines of watershed. The abundant supply of sediment through this time gradually lifted these floods upon the surface of thick and wide plains, sloping with the valleys. After the departure of the ice, the supply of both water and sediment was so diminished that the streams could no longer overspread these flood-plains and add to their depth, but were henceforth occupied mainly in slow excavation and removal of these deposits, leaving remnants of them as plains or terraces, often 100 to 200 feet, or more, above their present channel. The Loess bluffs bordering the Missouri river are of this origin. We have now to consider an area where such free drainage could not take place, because the descent of the land is northward, in the same direction with the retreat of the ice-sheet. As soon as this receded beyond the watershed dividing the basin of the Minnesota from that of the Red river, it is evident that a lake, fed by the glacial melting, stood at the

2

foot of the ice-fields, and extended northward as they withdrew along the valley of the Red river to Lake Winnipeg, filling this valley and its branches to the height of the lowest point over which an outlet could be found. Until the ice-barrier was melted upon the area now crossed by the Nelson river, thereby draining this glacial lake, its outlet was along the present course of the Minnesota river. At first its overflow was upon the nearly level undulating surface of the drift, 1100 to 1125 feet above sea, at the west side of Traverse and Big Stone counties ; but in process of time this cut a channel here 100 to 150 feet deep, the highest point of which is almost exactly 1000 feet above sea.* From this outlet the Red River valley, 30 to 50 miles wide, stretches 315 miles north to Lake Winnipeg, which is 710 feet above sea. Along this entire distance there is a very uniform continuous descent of a little less than one foot per mile. The drift contained in the ice-sheet upon this area, and the silt gathered by glacial rivers from each side, were here deposited in a lake, shallow near its mouth, but becoming gradually deeper northward. At the north line of the United States, its depth was 200 feet, and at Lake Winnipeg 300 feet. Beyond our national boundary, this lake covered a larger area, varying from 100 to 200 miles in breadth at and west of Lake Winnipeg ; and its total length appears to have been at least 600 miles. Because of its relation to the retreating continental ice-sheet, it is proposed to call this *Lake Agassiz*, in memory of the first prominent advocate of the theory that the drift was produced by land-ice.

The basin of Lake Agassiz, now drained in its southern portion by the Red river, has an exceedingly flat surface, sloping imperceptibly northward, as also from each side to its central line. The Red river has its course in this axial depression, where it has cut a channel 20 to 60 feet deep. It is bordered by only few and narrow areas of bottom-land, instead of which its banks usually rise steeply on one side and by moderate slopes on the other, to the lacustrine plain which thence reaches nearly level 10 to 25 miles from the river. Its tributaries cross the plain in similar channels, which, as also the Red river, have occasional gullies connected with them, dry through most of the year, varying from a few hundred feet to a mile or more in length. Between the drainage lines, areas often 5 to 15 miles wide remain unmarked by any water-courses. The highest portions of these tracts are commonly from 2 to 5 feet above the lowest. The material of the greater part of this ancient lake-bed is fine clayey silt, horizontally stratified ; but at its south end, in Traverse county and the south half of Wilkin county, it is mostly unstratified boulder-clay, which differs from the rolling or undulating unmodified drift of the adjoining region only in having its surface nearly flat. Both these formations are almost impervious to water, which therefore in the rainy season fills their shallow depressions, but none of these are so deep as to form permanent lakes. Even sloughs which continue marshy through the summer are infrequent, but, where they do occur cover large areas, usually several miles in extent. In crossing the vast plain of this valley on clear days, the higher land at its sides, and the groves along

---

* The height of Lake Traverse, according to leveling by United States engineers, in connection with Gen. Warren's survey of the Minnesota river, is 1900 feet. This is 8 feet above Big Stone lake, from which it is separated at the lowest place by only a slight watershed, perhaps five feet above Lake Traverse. Lake Winnipeg, by the survey of the Canadian Pacific railway, is 710 feet above sea.

its rivers are first seen in the distance as if their upper edges were raised a little above the horizon, with a very narrow strip of sky below. The first appearance of the tree-tops thus somewhat resembles that of dense flocks of birds flying very low several miles away. By rising a few feet, as from the ground to a wagon, or by nearer approach, the outlines become clearly defined as a grove, with a mere line of sky beneath it. Besides this mirage, the traveller is also reminded, in the same manner as at sea, that the earth is round. The surface of the plain is seen only for a distance of three or four miles; houses and grain-stacks have their tops visible first, after which, in approaching, they gradually come into full view; and the highlands, 10 or 15 miles away, forming the side of the valley, apparently lie beyond a wide depression, like a distant high coast.

In Clay county the east side of Lake Agassiz coincided nearly with the line between ranges 45 and 46. From the north line of the county to the North-ern Pacific railroad, the land rises about 300 feet in going a few miles east-ward, and thence stretches away 25 miles, everywhere slightly undulating, but with little change in its general height. In southern Clay county and at the east side of Wilkin county, the east shore of this glacial lake ran a few degrees east of south, to where it crosses the line of Otter Tail county, 10 miles west of Fergus Falls. Beyond this it has a south-east course about six miles to the Red river. At its east side along this distance, the glacial drift is rolling and hilly, as already described in connection with the moraine, which in south-western Otter Tail county is only 8 to 10 miles east of this basin. From the Red river the lake shore ran southward through Western township; thence in Grant county it appears to curve to the south-east, south and south-west. It crosses the railroad about a mile north-west of Herman, and its further course is by a curve south-west, west, and north-west, passing through the south-east part of Traverse county, and coming to Lake Traverse at its bluffs on the south side of the Mustinka river. Red and Bois des Sioux rivers lie 15 to 20 miles west of this shore-line.

Beaches and deltas, as well as the change from a smoothed to an undulating surface, mark the border of this lacustrine area. At and west of Muskoda, the Northern Pacific railroad cuts through a thick and extensive deposit of sand, with beds of gravel and clay in some portions, constituting a plain one and a half miles wide. This extends two or three miles to the north, and is also represented by similar accumulations south of the Buffalo river, which here enters the area formerly covered by Lake Agassiz. These beds have their surface 1075 to 1100 feet above sea, being 100 feet below the adjoining uplands on the east, and 150 feet above the lacustrine plain, which begins two miles farther west and extends 15 miles to the Red river. They appear to be the delta brought down by the Buffalo river and spread in the side of the lake at its mouth. Since the drainage of the lake the river has excavated a large gap through this deposit. A sixth of a mile east of Mus-koda station, at the east edge of the delta-plain, is a ridge of interbedded gravel and sand, 25 rods wide and 10 feet high, with its top about 1110 feet above sea. A fine section is exposed by its excavation for railroad ballast, showing the stratification to be mainly level, but inclined at the sides par-allel with the gently sloping surface. This beach ridge or bar extends about a half mile from north to south. It is separated from the higher land east-ward by a depression about 10 feet deep and a quarter of a mile wide. Marginal deposits of considerable extent, like the plain of Muskoda, are only found where some stream entered the lake; but beach ridges, similar to the foregoing, were noted at several places in crossing the shore-line of this lake, and, when attention is given to tracing them, will probably be found continuous through long distances. Such a ridge crosses the north line of Wilkin county near the north-west corner of sec. 4, t. 136, r. 45, extending at least one and a half miles from north to south. It was again crossed near the south-east corner of sec. 21, Western, where the road from Fergus Falls to Campbell turns from a south-west to a more nearly west course. Here the ascent from its east side is 10 feet, and the descent at the west about 20. The width of the ridge, including its slopes, is 20 or 25 rods. About a mile farther west the road crosses a second ridge of half this size, about 20 feet below the first. One and a half miles north-west from Herman is a beach-ridge 15 feet above the lacustrine plain at its north-west side. The depression south-east of it is 6 or 7 feet deep and 30 rods wide, and from this there is an ascent of about 15 feet to the plain of Herman, which was therefore above the level of the lake when this beach was formed. Three miles farther north-west (at the 183rd mile-post of the railroad) is a smaller beach-ridge. The top of this is about 1035, and of that near Herman about 1055 feet above sea. All these beaches consist of sand and water-worn gravel; and in Western and Herman it is noteworthy that all the adjoining areas are boulder clay. It is expected that a full exploration of these shore-lines will be made before the completion of this survey, so that the final report shall contain a map of this lake, so far as it lay within the limits of Minnesota.

The Outlet of Lake Agassiz. The excavation of the remarkable valley occupied by the Minnesota river was first explained in 1868 by Gen. G. K. Warren, who attributed it to the outflow from this ancient lake that filled the basin of Red river and Lake Winnipeg. This valley or channel begins at the northern part of Lake Traverse, and first extends south-west to the head of this lake, thence south-east to Mankato, and next north and north-east to the Mississippi at Fort Snelling, its length being about 250 miles. Its width varies from one to four miles, and its depth is from 100 to 225 feet. The country through which it lies, as far as to Carver, about 25 miles above its junction with the Mississippi, is a nearly level expanse of till, only moderately undulating, with no prominent hills or notable depressions, excepting this deep channel and those formed by its tributary streams. Below Carver it intersects the hilly morainic belt which has been already described. Its entire course is through a region of unmodified drift, which has no exposures of solid rock at its surface within' long distances upon each side. Probably no other channel of equal extent and depth has been eroded in till upon either this or the old continent.

Bluffs in slopes from 20° to 40°, and rising 100 to 200 feet to the general level of the country, form the sides of this trough-like valley. They have been produced by the washing away of their base, leaving the upper portion to fall down and thus take its steep slopes. The river in deepening its channel has been constantly changing its course, so that its current has been turned alternately against the opposite sides of its valley, at some time undermining every portion of them. In a few places this process is still going forward, but mainly the course of the Minnesota river is in the bottom-land, which descends in gentle or often broken slopes 10 to 40 or 50 feet within one fourth to one half mile from the foot of the bluffs; then becoming the present flood-plain, one eighth to one half mile, or rarely one mile or more. in width, with its height 5 or 10 feet above ordinary low water. Comparatively little excavation has been done by the present river. As we approach its source, it dwindles to a small stream, flowing through long lakes, and we finally pass to Lake Traverse, which empties northward; yet along the upper Minnesota and at the divide between this and Red river, this valley or channel and its enclosing bluffs are as remarkable as along the lower part of Minnesota river. It is thus clearly shown to have been the outlet of Lake Agassiz, excavated while the melting ice-sheet supplied extraordinary floods, much greater in volume than the combined waters of the Minnesota and Nelson rivers at the present time.

This valley in many places cuts through the sheet of drift, and reaches the underlying rocks, which have frequent exposures along its entire course below Big Stone lake. Their contour is much more uneven than that of the drift. In the 100 miles from Big Stone lake to Fort Ridgely the strata are metamorphic gneisses and granites, which often fill the entire valley, one to two miles wide, rising in a profusion of knolls and hills, 50 to 100 feet above the river. The depth eroded has been limited here by the presence of these rocks, among which the river flows in a winding course, crossing them at many places in rapids or falls. From New Ulm to its mouth the river is at many places bordered by Cretaceous and Lower Silurian rocks, which are nearly level in stratification. These vary in height from a few feet to 50 or rarely 75 or 100 feet above the river. From Mankato to Ottawa the river occupies a valley cut in Shakopee limestone underlain by Jordan sandstone, which form frequent bluffs upon both sides, 50 to 75 feet high. After excavating the overlying 125 to 150 feet of till, the river here found a former valley, eroded by pre-glacial streams. Its bordering walls of rock, varying from one fourth mile to at least two miles apart, are in many portions of this distance concealed by drift, which alone forms one or both sides of the valley. The next point at which the river is seen to be enclosed by rock-walls, is in its last two miles, where it flows between bluffs of Trenton limestone underlain by St. Peter sandstone, 100 feet high, and about a mile apart. This also is a pre-glacial channel, its farther continuation being occupied by the Mississippi river. The only erosion effected by the Minnesota river here since the glacial period has been to clear away a part of the drift with which the valley was then filled. Its depth at some earlier time was much greater than now, as shown by the salt-well on the bottom-land of the Minnesota river at Belle Plaine, where 202 feet of stratified gravel, sand and clay were penetratad before reaching the rock. The bottom of the pre-glacial channel there is thus at least 175 feet lower than the mouth of the Minnesota river. The excavation of the drift down to the old rocks by the outflow from Lake Agassiz, enables us to estimate approximately the depth of the general drift-sheet upon this part of Minnesota. It probably averages about 150 feet.

Heights of the bluffs, which form the sides of this valley, composed of till enclosing layers of gravel and sand in some places, and frequently having rock at their base, are as follows, stated in feet above the lakes and river: along the south part of Lake Traverse, 100 to 125; at Brown's Valley and along Big Stone lake, mainly about 125, the highest portions reaching 150;

at Ortonville, 130; at Lac qui Parle and Montevideo, 100; at Granite Falls, 150; at Minnesota Falls, 165; thence to Redwood Falls, Fort Ridgely and New Ulm, 165 to 180; at Mankato 200 to 225; at St. Peter and Ottawa, 220 to 230; at LeSueur and Henderson, 210 to 225; at Belle Plaine and Jordan, about 230; and at Shakopee 210 to 220. The morainic hills through which this valley extends below Shakopee are 225 to 250 feet in height. The elevation of Minnesota river above the sea is given on a following page. The expanse of till through which this channel is eroded slopes from 1125 feet above sea at Big Stone lake to 975 at Mankato, in 140 miles; and thence it descends to 925 at Shakopee, in 50 miles. This channel, as far as to Mankato, lies nearly, midway between the terminal moraine previously described and the Coteau des Prairies, toward each of which there is a very slight ascent, sufficient to cause drainage to follow this central line.

Lakes Traverse and Big Stone are from one to one and a half miles wide, mainly occupying the entire area between the bases of the bluffs. Lake Traverse is 23 miles long; it is mostly less than 10 feet deep, and its greatest depth probably does not reach 20 feet. Big Stone lake is 26 miles long, and its greatest depth is reported to be from 15 to 30 feet. The portion of the channel between these lakes is widely known as Brown's Valley. As we stand upon the bluffs here, looking down 125 feet on these long and narrow lakes in their trough-like valley, which extends across the five miles between them, where the basins of Hudson bay and the Gulf of Mexico are now divided, we have nearly the picture which was presented when the melting ice-sheet of British America was pouring its floods along this hollow. Then the entire extent of the valley was doubtless filled every summer by a river which covered all the present areas of flood-plain, in many places occupying as great width as these lakes.

Gen. Warren observes that Lake Traverse is probably due to a partial silting up of the channel since the outflow from the Red River basin ceased, the Minnesota river at the south having brought in sufficient alluvium to form a dam; while Big Stone lake is similarly referred to the sediment brought into the valley just below it by Whetstone river. The deep, winding channel of the Whetstone river near its mouth is quite remarkable; and its level alluvium, about 5 feet above the lake, fills the valley, a mile wide between Big Stone City and Ortonville.

Fifteen miles below Big Stone lake, the Minnesota river flows through a marshy lake four miles long and about a mile wide. This may be due to the accumulation of alluvium brought into the valley by the Pomme de Terre river, which has its mouth about two miles below. Twenty-five miles from Big Stone lake, the river enters Lac qui Parle, which extends 8 miles, with a width varying from one-half to three-fourths of a mile and a maximum depth of 12 feet. This lake, as Gen. Warren suggests, has been formed by a barrier of stratified sand and silt which the Lac qui Parle river has thrown across the valley. He also shows that Lake Pepin on the Mississippi is dammed in the same way by the sediment of the Chippewa river; and that Lake St. Croix and the last 30 miles of the Minnesota river are similarly held as level back-water by the recent deposits of the Mississippi.

All the tributaries of the Minnesota river have cut deeply into the drift, because the main valley has given them the requisite slope. The largest of these extend many miles, and have their mouths level with the bottom-land of the Minnesota river. The bluffs of all these valleys are also everywhere seamed and gullied by frequent rills and springs, many of which flow only after rains. Few of the large inlets have any great amount of sediment deposited opposite their mouths, showing that their excavation was mostly done at the same time with that of the main valley. The short ravines are more recent in their origin, and the material that filled their place is commonly spread in fan-shaped, moderately sloping banks below their mouths, which are thus kept at a height from 30 to 40 feet above the present flood-plain. The road from Fort Ridgely to New Ulm runs along the side of the bluff at the only height where a nearly level straight course could be obtained, being just above these deposits and below the ravines.

The valleys of the Pomme de Terre and Chippewa rivers, 75 to 100 feet deep along most of their course, and one-fourth mile to one mile in width, were probably avenues of drainage from the melting ice-fields in their north-ward retreat. Between these rivers, in the 22 miles from Appleton to Monte-video, the glacial floods at first flowed in several channels, which are excavated 40 to 80 feet below the general level of the drift-sheet, and vary from one-eighth to one-half mile in width. One of these, starting from the bend of the Pomme de Terre river, 1½ miles east of Appleton, extends 15 miles south-east to the Chippewa river near the center of Tunsburg. This old channel is joined at Milan station by another, which branches off from the Minnesota valley, running four miles east-south-east; it is also joined at the north-west corner of Tunsburg by a very notable channel which extends eastward from the middle of Lac qui Parle. The latter channel, and its continuation in the old Pomme de Terre valley to the Chippewa river, are excavated nearly as deep as the channel occupied by the Minnesota river. Its west portion holds a marsh generally known as the "Big Slough." Lac qui Parle would have to be raised only a few feet to turn it through this deserted valley. The only other localities where we have proof that the outflow from Lake Agassiz had more than one channel are 7 and 10 miles below Big Stone lake, where isolated remnants of the general sheet of till occur south of Odessa station and again three miles south-east. Each of these former islands is about a mile long, and rises 75 feet above the sur-rounding low land, or nearly as high as the bluffs enclosing the valley, which here measures four miles across, having a greater width than at any other point.

ELEVATIONS.

In connection with the foregoing description of topographic features, it seems desirable to present the series of altitudes which have been deter-mined in this region by railroad and other surveys. They are mostly copied from Prof. Winchell's first annual report as geologist of Minnesota, in which they were referred to Lake Superior as a datum, calling it 600 feet above sea. Since that publication, the researches of Messrs. Gardner and Gannett, of the U. S. Geological Survey of the Territories, have shown the height of Lake Superior to be 609.4 feet above mean tide. The correction which this requires is adopted in the following tables; and in those gathered from later reports a few other changes are made, as called for by determin-ations of other datum points, mainly following Gannett's *Lists of Elevations*, fourth edition. These heights are stated in feet above mean sea-level :

Northern Pacific Railroad.

Lake Superior,	609.4	Audubon,	1317
Brainerd,	1214	Lake Park,	1342
Mississippi river (bed),	1147	Hawley,	1159
Wadena,	1358	Muskoda,	1092
Leaf river (bed),	1316	Buffalo river (bed),	947
New York Mills,	1418	Glyndon,	932
Otter Tail river (bed),	1327	Moorhead,	913
Perham,	1375	Red river, low water,	851
Hobart,	1393	Red river, high water	885
Pelican river (bed)	1346	Fargo,	912
Detroit,	1371	Jamestown,	1415
Oak Lake station,	1376	Missouri river, at Bismarck,	1649

St. Paul, Minneapolis & Manitoba Railroad.

a. From St. Cloud to St. Vincent.

East Saint Cloud,	1020	Red river, at Dayton bridge,	1071
Mississippi river, low water,	962	Creek-bed near Barnesville,	997
West Saint Cloud,	1034	Track on bridge here,	1012
Osakis,	1337	Glyndon,	932
Victoria,	1375	Buffalo river, track,	928
Alexandria,	1391	Buffalo river, water,	915
Ida,	1411	Averill,	927
Chippewa river, track,	1369	Felton,	925
Chippewa river, water,	1339	Borup,	921
Evansville,	1354	Wild Rice river, track,	919
Summit, 1 m. beyond last,	1378	Wild Rice river, water,	910
Christina,	1228	Red Lake river, track,	857
St. Olaf,	1344	Red Lake river, water,	850
Summit, 2½ m. beyond last,	1366	Saint Vincent,	801
Pomme de Terre river, track,	1239	Red river, low water,	767
Pomme de Terre river, water,	1205	Red river, high water,	796

b.—From St. Paul to Breckenridge.

Saint Paul,	698.4	Benson,	1042
Minneapolis,	830	Chippewa river, track,	1030
Lake Minnetonka, water,	922	Chippewa river, water,	1021
Delano,	923	Clontarf,	1041
Waverly,	1007	Hancock,	1150
Twelve Mile Creek,	995	Summit, 1½ miles beyond last,	1167
Howard Lake sta.,	1049	Pomme de Terre river, track,	1073
Smith Lake sta.,	1049	Pomme de Terre river, water,	1062
Cokato,	1022	Morris,	1122
Darwin,	1127	Summit, 2 miles beyond last,	1151
Litchfield,	1125	Donnelly,	1121
Swede Grove,	1186	Herman,	1063
Atwater,	1207	Mustinka creek,	1021
Summit, 4½ miles beyond last,	1264	Gorton,	1017
Kandiyohi,	1216	Tintah,	991
Willmar,	1124	Campbell,	977
St. John's,	1116	Doran,	968
Kirkhoven,	1104	Breckenridge,	957
De Graff,	1056		

Hastings & Dakota Railroad.

(Corrected at and west of Shakopee to agree with the height of Minnesota river at tha place.)

Hastings,	709.4	Chaska,	740
Farmington,	900.6	Carver,	827
Prior Lake sta.,	954	Dahlgren,	994
Prior Lake, water,	914	Benton,	959
Shakopee,	768	Young America,	1002
Minnesota river, low water,	704.5	Tiger lake, water,	991
Minnesota river, high water,	731	Glencoe,	1015

Winona & St. Peter Railroad.

Winona,	652.65	Oshawa,	980
Lewiston,	1211	Nicollet,	978
Rochester,	990	Minnesota river, high water,	808
Owatonna,	1047	New Ulm,	835
Mankato,	779	Sleepy Eye,	1032
Kasota,	837	Marshall,	1173
St. Peter,	810	State line,	1475
Minnesota river, high water,	754	Summit of Coteau, 22 ms. W.,	1999

St. Paul & Sioux City Railroad.

The profile of this line, stated on p. 38 of Gannett's *Lists of Elevations*, and derived from the first annual report on the Geology of Minnesota, is 50 feet, approximately, too high, as compared with the determination of Minnesota river by the U. S. Engineer Corps.

Survey for Minnesota Northern Railroad.

Wadena,	1358	Bass lake,	1333
Pease Prairie, t. 133, r. 38,	1459	Red river at Fergus Falls,	1181
Clitherall lake,	1341	Top of dam at Pelican Rapids,	1311
Turtle lake,	1331		

Survey for Hutchinson Branch of the Minneapolis & Northwestern Railway.

Top of Watertown dam,	925	Swan lake,	1045
Ocean marsh, 7 ms. W.,	997	Crow river, low water,	1029
Winsted lake,	994	Hutchinson,	1042

Mississippi River.

Lake Itasca,	1575	Lake City, low water,	664.2
Mouth of Leech Lake river,	1356	Winona, low water,	639.9
Mouth of Sandy Lake river,	1253	La Crosse, low water,	626.3
Mouth of Crow Wing river,	1130	Dubuque, low water,	599.1
At head of Sauk Rapids,	991	Keokuk, low water of 1851,	481.8
Saint Cloud, low water,	962	Keokuk, high water of 1851,	502.5
Top of Saint Anthony's falls, low water,	800	Saint Louis, low water,	394.5
One-half mile below Saint Anthony's falls, low water,	721	Saint Louis, high water of 1844	435.9
		Cairo, ordinary low water,	291.2
Mouth of Minnesota river, low water,	704.4	Cairo, low water of 1871,	279.3
		Cairo, high water of 1867,	333
Saint Paul, low water,	685.4	Memphis, low water,	184
Saint Paul, high water,	706.4	Memphis, high water,	219
Hastings, low water,	670.5	Natchez, low water,	66
		Baton Rouge, low water,	34

Minnesota River, low-water slope.

(Levels by U. S. Engineer Corps.)

Big Stone lake,	992.60	Mankato,	765.7
Pomme de Terre river,	962.68	Saint Peter,	743.4
Lac qui Parle,	954.04	Ottawa, ♠	736
Chippewa river,	939.84	LeSueur,	729.2
Foot of Minnesota Falls	883.14	East Henderson,	724.8
Yellow Medicine river,	875.12	Henderson,	723.4
Redwood river,	831.67	Faxon,	713.4
Fort Ridgely,	807.39	Belle Plaine,	709.8
Big Cottonwood river,	795.92	Crest of Little Rapids,	706
Judson,	773.78	Foot of Little Rapids,	704.8
South Bend,	769.2	Mouth,	704.4
Blue Earth river,	768.9		

Red River of the North.

Lake Traverse,	1000.5	Moorhead, low water,	851
Otter Tail lake,	1325	Moorhead, high water,	885
Fergus Falls,	1181	Saint Vincent, low water,	767
Dayton bridge,	1071	Saint Vincent, high water,	796
Breckenridge,	940	Lake Winnipeg,	710

The Great Lakes.

Superior,	609.40	Erie,	573.08
Michigan and Huron,	589.15	Ontario,	250

FOREST AND PRAIRIE.

A considerable part of the area included under this report is well timbered. These forests at their borders and around the few prairies which they enclose, become gradually more open with fewer and smaller trees, or form scattered groves, with intervening bushes or grass-land. The wooded part of this district is its north-east and east side, and takes in nearly all of Becker and Otter Tail counties, in which its west boundary extends from the White Earth Agency south to the Northern Pacific railroad; thence west by Audubon, and then south by Cormorant, Pelican, Lizzie and Prairie lakes; in Erhard's Grove and Elizabeth, it includes a few miles on the west side of Pelican river; and next bends south eastward, passing by the north side of Fergus Falls, to Wall lake and the north edge of St. Olaf. Through the center of Otter Tail county the woods of its east and west portions are divided by a nearly continuous belt destitute of forest, averaging about six miles wide, which reaches from Lake Christina to Clitherall, Otter Tail and Rush lakes, and onward by Perham to the North line of the county. About half of Douglas county is forest, very irregularly bounded, its south-west limit being in the vicinity of Lakes Oscar and Mary. Pope county has only scattered groves, sometimes one or two miles wide, but separated from each other by yet wider areas of prairie, which include probably nineteen-twentieths of the county. Kandiyohi county has an area of forest 15 miles long from west to east and 3 to 10 miles wide, lying north-west, north and north-east of Green lake; also, groves of small extent, found frequently on the borders of lakes in all parts of the county except its south-west quarter.

The Big Woods. In Meeker county and others at the east and south-east, a belt of timber about 45 miles wide extends nearly one hundred miles from north to south, commonly called the "Big Woods." Like the woods of Becker, Otter Tail and Douglas counties, it is connected northward with the great forest that overspreads nearly all of northern and north-eastern Minnesota. The west border of the Big Woods crosses Meeker county in an irregular line that has frequent indentations and spurs, passing from the northwest corner of the county south-east and south by Manannah, Forest City and Darwin, to Greenleaf. This boundary between forest on the east and prairie on the west, enters McLeod county at its north-west corner, and runs south-eastward across this and Sibley counties, by Hutchinson, Glencoe, New Auburn and Arlington. Through Nicollet county the forest occupies a width of two to four miles along the west side of Minnesota river to Mankato and South Bend. It also extends in about the same amount along the north side of Minnesota river for 15 miles above Mankato; and Timber lake, 6 miles north-west from St. Peter, is bordered by broad wood lands.

East of this line, the Big woods cover all of Wright, Carver, Scott and Le Sueur counties, excepting small enclosed prairies and the bottom-lands and terraces of modified drift within the valley of the Minnesota river. Beyond South Bend the boundary of this timbered belt is a few miles outside the limit of my exploration. Prof. Winchell, in a former report, states that its course bends eastward in Blue Earth county, passing near Janesville, and about six miles north of Waseca. Thence it turns north-east to Faribault and Cannon City, from which a spur of forest reaches south along the east side of Straight river to Owatonna. The east border of the Big Woods has a nearly north course, passing from Cannon City to Northfield, Lakeville, and the west edge of Minneapolis.

Limits of Species. Many trees, shrubs and herbs that flourish northward, have their southern limit at a line north-east and north of the Big Woods; while the forest of Becker, Otter Tail and Douglas counties contains them only in its north-east part. Among these northern species are white, red and gray pines, black spruce, balsam fir, low blueberry, and cranberry. Most of these were seen in the township of Spruce Hill at the north east corner of Douglas county, which seems to be their only occurrence in that county. Thence they are found sparingly northward to the Northern Pacific railroad, beyond which are valuable pineries, beginning at New York Mills, Pine lakes, and Frazee City, and extending indefinitely to the north and north-east. None of these species are found in the Big Woods, which however contain others, as cottonwood, bitternut, wild crab-apple, and frost grape, that are rare or wanting in the northern forest.

List of Trees and Shrubs. The following species of trees and shrubs have been observed in Becker and Otter Tail counties, by Mr. R. L. Frazee, manufacturer of lumber at Frazee City, Becker county: white pine (*Pinus Strobus*, L.), red (commonly called Norway) pine (*P. resinosa*, Ait.), and gray or Banks' pine, often called "jack pine" (*P. Banksiana*, Lambert), black spruce (*Abies nigra*, Poir.), balsam fir (*Abies balsamea*, Marshall), balsam poplar (*Populus balsamifera*, L.), paper or canoe birch (*Betula papyracea*, Ait.), and beaked hazelnut (*Corylus rostrata*, Ait.), common north-east from the Northern Pacific railroad; white elm (*Ulmus Americana*, L.), bass (*Tilia Americana*, L.), sugar maple (*Acer saccharinum*, Wang.), box-elder (*Negundo aceroides*, Mœnch), black ash (*Fraxinus sambucifolia*, Lam.), bur and white oak (*Quercus macrocarpa*, Michx., and *Q. alba*, L.), ironwood (*Ostrya Vir-*

ginica, Willd.), species of willow (*Salix*), poplar or aspen (*Populus tremuloides,* Michx.), tamarack (*Larix Americana,* Michx.), prickly ash (*Zanthoxylum Americanum,* Mill.), smooth sumac (*Rhus glabra,* L.), climbing bittersweet (*Celastrus scandens,* L.), wild plum, wild red cheŕy and choke cherry (*Prunus Americana,* Marshall, *P. Pennsylvanica,* L., and *P. Virginiana,* L.), ninebark (*Spiræa opulifolia,* L.), raspberry and high blackberry (*Rubus strigosus,* Michx., and *R. villosus,* Ait.), thorn (*Cratægus,*) Juneberry (*Amelanchier Canadensis,* T. & G.), prickly and smooth gooseberries (*Ribes Cynosbati,* L., and *R. hirtellum,* Michx.,) black currant (*Ribes floridum,* L.), wolfberry (*Symphoricarpus occidentalis,* R. Brown), high bush cranberry (*Viburnum Opulus,* L.), and hazelnut (*Corylus Americana,* Walt.) common generally ; slippery or red elm (*Ulmus fulva,* Micheli), black oak (*Q. coccinea,* var *tinctoria*), large-toothed poplar (*P. grandidentata,* Michx.), and black cherry (*P. serotina,* Ehrhart), less frequent ; red oak (*Q. rubra,* L.), soft or red maple (*Acer rubrum,* L.), black raspberries (*Rubus occidentalis,* L.), and elder (*Sambucus Canadensis,* L.), scarce ; cottonwood (*populus monilifera,* Ait.), seen rarely about the shores of lakes ; and hackberry (*Celtis occidentalis,* L.), known only at one place, near Lake Lida.

The Big Woods are principally made up of the following species of trees : white or American elm, bass, sugar maple, black and bur oaks, butternut, slippery or red elm, soft or red maple, bitternut, white and black ash, ironwood, wild plum, Juneberry, American crab-apple, common poplar or aspen, large-toothed poplar, tamarack (in swamps), box-elder, black cherry, cottonwood (beside rivers and lakes), water beech, willows, hackberry, paper or canoe birch, white oak, and red cedar. This list, in which the arrangement is according to the estimated order of abundance, is given by Prof. Winchell for Hennepin county, in his fifth annual report, p. 142 ; but it appears to be applicable, with slight differences, to all other portions of the Big Woods. Everywhere through this forest the two largest and most plentiful species are elm and bass. Another list of trees and shrubs, noted in passing through these woods in Scott county, is recorded by Prof. Winchell in his second annual report, pp. 210 and 211 ; followed by a few additional species, as the Kentucky coffee-tree, black walnut, and yellow birch, seen in ascending the valley of the Minnesota river to Big Stone lake.

Timber is found along the Minnesota river in a nearly continuous, though often very narrow strip, bordering the river through almost its entire course ; but generally leaving much of the bottom-land treeless. The bluffs on the north-east side of the river have for the most part only thin and scanty groves or scattered trees. The south-western bluffs, on the contrary, are heavily wooded through Blue Earth and Brown counties, excepting two or three miles at New Ulm. They also are frequently well timbered in Redwood and Yellow Medicine counties ; but in Lac qui Parle county they are mostly treeless, and have only occasional groves. The greater abundance of timber on the south-western bluffs appears to be due to their being less exposed to the sun, and therefore more moist, than the bluffs at the opposite side of the valley. Above Montevideo the timber is mainly restricted to a narrow belt beside the river, and to tributary valleys and ravines.

About Big Stone lake, timber generally fringes the shore ; occurs of larger growth in the ravines of its bluffs ; and covers its islands, situated within six miles above its mouth. The speceies of trees observed by Prof. Winchell near the foot of this lake on its north-east side, are the following in their order of abundance : white ash, bur-oak, bass, white elm, box-elder, cotton-wood, hackberry, ironwood, soft maple, wild plum, slippery elm, and willow. The shrubs recorded in the same locality are grape, prickly and smooth gooseberries, wolfberry, black currant, prickly ash, red and black raspberries, elder, sweet viburnum, red-osier dogwood, climbing bittersweet, choke cherry, red and white rose, Virginia creeper, waahoo, and smooth sumac.

Red river has no timber, or very little, for twenty miles east from Breck-enridge. In the ten miles next below Breckenridge, it is bordered by scat-tered groves of bur-oak, ash, box-elder, elm, and bass, occupying perhaps one-fourth of this distance, while small poplars and willows occasionally appear in the spaces between the groves. Farther to the north, this river is continuously fringed with timber, and its larger tributaries have their course marked in the same way. The growth of wood is here confined to the banks of the streams, which have cut hollows 20 to 40 feet deep in the broad lacustrine plain. The trees and shrubs which thus occur along the Red and Buffalo rivers in northwestern Clay county, are stated by Mr. Adam Stein, of Georgetown, to be the following : white ash, white and slippery elm, bur-oak, ironwood, poplar, box-elder, wild plum, hackberry, prickly ash, frost grape, choke cherry, red raspberry, rose, thorn, prickly and smooth goosberries, black currant, and hazelnut, more or less common ; wild red cherry, Juneberry, high bush cranberry, and cottonwood, rare.

Prairies. The greater part of the region here reported is prairie. This term is commonly used to embrace all tracts destitute of trees and shrubs but well covered with grass. Groves of a few acres, or sometimes a hundred acres or more, occur here and there upon this area beside lakes, and a nar-row line of timber often borders streams, as just described along the Minne-sota and Red rivers ; but many lakes and streams have neither bush nor tree in sight, and frequently none is visible in a view which ranges from five to ten miles in all directions. Most of these prairies have the moderately undulating contour described at the beginning of our remarks on topography. Within the area of Lake Agassiz the surface is almost absolutely level. Other portions of these prairies are quite hilly, having undulations of 100 feet or more, as from Hawley southward along the east side of the lacustrine area to Red river ; thence south-east to Pelican lake and Lake Oscar ; the morainic hills of Pope county ; and parts of Acton, Danielson, and Green-leaf, in Meeker county. If we compare the forests with the prairies as to their prevailing contour, we find that for the most part the former are hilly and the latter gently undulating ; yet much of the timbered areas, especially of the Big Woods, is only slightly uneven and occasionally quite level, while some very hilly tracts are prairies. The material of nearly all these areas is closely alike, being till or unmodified glacial drift, showing no important differences such as might cause the growth of forest in one region and of only grass and herbage in another.

The absence of trees and shrubs upon large areas, called prairies, in this and neighboring states, is generally attributed correctly to the effect of fires. Through many centuries fires have almost annually swept over these areas, generally destroying all seedling trees and shrubs, and sometimes extending the border of the prairie by adding tracts from which the forest had been burned. Late in autumn and again in the spring the dead grass of the prairie burns very rapidly, so that a fire within a few days sometimes spreads fifty or a hundred miles. The groves that remain in the prairie region are usually in a more or less sheltered position, being on the border of lakes and streams and sometimes nearly surrounded by them; while areas that cannot be reached by fires, as islands, are almost always wooded. If fires should fail to overrun the prairies in the future, it can hardly be doubted that nearly all of them would gradually and slowly be changed to forest. Yet it does not appear that fires in forests at the West are more frequent or destructive than at the East, and our inquiry must go back a step further to ask why fires east of the Appalachian Mountains had nowhere exterminated the forest, while so extensive areas of prairie were produced by them in the West. Among the conditions which have led to this difference, we must probably place first the generally greater amount, and somewhat more equal distribution throughout the year, of rain in the eastern states.

The average growth on the dry portions of the prairies of this region would make about a half a ton of hay per acre. It affords magnificent pasturage, but the pioneer farmer gathers nearly all his hay from the frequent depressions or "sloughs," which yield twice as much as the higher land, but of somewhat inferior quality. These are marshes through the spring and early summer, but become mostly dry later in the season, so that horses can be driven across them.

The most abundant grasses found upon the prairies in the vicinity of New Ulm by Mr. B. Juni of that place, are as follows: *Andropogon furcatus*, Muhl., *Sorghum nutans*, Gray, *Bouteloua curtipendula*, Gray, and *Stipa spartea*, Trin., common on portions neither very dry nor very moist; *Andropogon scoparius*, Michx., and *Bouteloua hirsuta*, Lagasca, common on dry swells; *Spartina cynosuroides*, Willd., in sloughs, making the principal mass of their hay; *Leersia oryzoides*, Swartz, with the last; and the stout *Phragmites communis*, Trin., common on the marshy shores of lakelets. The prairies also bear a great variety of flowers. Of asters Mr. Juni finds the most common species to be *Aster surculosus*, Michx., *A. sericeus*, Vent., and *A. Tradescanti*, L.; of golden-rod (*Solidago*), *S. Ohioensis*, Riddell, *S. Canadensis*, L., and *S. lanceolata*, L. Among the most noticeable and common plants of the prairies, besides the foregoing, are *Liatris spicata*, Willd., *Psoralea argophylla*, Pursh, *Petalostemon violaceus*, Michx., *P. candidus*, Michx., *Amorpha canescens*, Nutt.,[Rosa lucida*, Ehrhart, *Campanula rotundifolia*, L., *Phlox pilosa*, L., *Gentiana crinita*, Frœl., *G. detonsa*, Fries., and *Lilium Philadelphicum*, L.

STRATIGRAPHIC GEOLOGY.

My only observations of rocks older than the drift are confined to the deep valley of the Minnesota river, the topography of which has been already described. The only other exposure of the old rocks known within this area of 16,000 square miles is recorded by Owen, and was seen in his boat journey down the Red river, at a point a little above Fergus Falls. The geology of the Minnesota valley was explored by William H. Keating in 1823; by G. W. Featherstonhaugh in 1835; and by B. F. Shumard in 1848. Soon after the establishment of the present survey, Prof. Winchell in 1873 examined this valley throughout, and his description of it, embracing also notes as to the observations of these earlier explorers, occupies pages 127 to

212 of the second annual report. This treats very fully and completely of all the rock-formations of this valley; and its conclusions have been uniformly confirmed, while indeed very little important information has been added by my journey over the same ground.

The following description of the old rocks is therefore based in large part upon Prof. Winchell's report. They are taken up in their order of age, beginning with the oldest, and including metamorphic granites and gneisses of the great series denominated Eozoic or Archæan; a conglomerate and quartzite, considered of the same age with the Potsdam sandstone; the St. Lawrence limestone, Jordan sandstone, and Shakopee limestone, belonging to the Lower Magnesian or Calciferous epoch, all these above the metamorphic rocks being of the great Lower Silurian series; and various shales, sandstones, limestones, and clays, the latter sometimes holding beds of lignite, regarded together as of Cretaceous age. The St. Peter sandstone and Trenton limestone, of the Lower Silurian series and lying next above the Shakopee limestone, occur in this valley near its mouth, but not within the limits of the counties here reported. The glacial and modified drift come last in this order, being our latest completed geological formation.

Granites and Gneisses. These are metamorphic rocks of the series called Eozoic or Archæan, the most ancient known to geology. They are doubtless an extension from the large area of these rocks in north-eastern Minnesota. They are, however, generally covered by drift except in the counties which border Lake Superior, and have only few exposures in the central part of the State. The nearest of these are in the vicinity of St. Cloud, 75 miles from the Minnesota river. It has been already stated that the various rock-formations seen along this river have been uncovered by the excavation of a deep channel through the drift.

The granites and associated rocks of this valley occur frequently through a distance of 100 miles, from a point one mile below the mouth of Big Stone lake to about five miles south-east from Fort Ridgely. In the next 13 miles, no rocks older than the Cretaceous are found. Then comes the last outcrop of granite, opposite the south-east part of New Ulm, succeeded by conglomerate and quartzyte.

No rocks older than drift, excepting some Cretaceous deposits, occur in this valley along Traverse and Big Stone lakes, or in the distance between them. One mile below Big Stone lake, a coarse red granite begins and thence occupies nearly the whole valley for three miles, its highest portions rising 50 to 75 feet above the river. It again appears in low outcrops two and three miles from the last, in secs. 30 and 32, t. 121, r. 45, the first of these being on the north side of the Minnesota a little west of Stony Run, and the second on the south side at Mr. Frederick Frankhaus', a half mile west from the ford. Two to six miles south-east from the ford, in t. 120, r. 45, which extends from the mouth of Yellow Banks river to Marsh lake, similar granite, principally red or flesh-colored but in some portions light gray, forms abundant outcrops, mainly on the south side of the river, rising 50 to 75 feet in their highest portions. North of these, two ledges of this rock were noted about a mile apart, halfway between Odessa and Correll stations, the west one lying a little south of the railroad, while the east one is crossed by it. All the foregoing exposures are massive granite, containing a large proportion of feldspar to which its prevailing reddish color is due.

It is variously jointed, but does not exhibit the lamination which is generally noticeable in the south-eastward continuation of these rocks.

Gneiss has the same composition with granite, being made up of quartz, feldspar, and mica. It differs from granite in having these minerals laminated, or arranged more or less distinctly in layers. Nearly all the metamorphic rocks that remain to be described are varieties of gneiss, with which masses of granite, syenite, and hornblende schist occur rarely. For 15 miles from the upper part of Marsh lake to the middle of Lac qui Parle, we have no report of ledges. In sec. 32, t. 119, r. 42, an island of rock occurs in Lac qui Parle, and two ledges were seen across the lake on its west side. About two miles south-east, or one and a half miles above the foot of the lake, are several small and low exposures of rock, occuring at each side and also as islands. On the north-east side this is gneiss, mostly with N. E. to S. W. strike. Its dip was clearly shown at only one place, being there 75° S. E.

In the deserted channel between Lac qui Parle and the Chippewa river rock is exposed near the south-east corner of sec. 6, Tunsburg. It also occurs at the south east corner of this township, in the bottom-land on the east side of the Chippewa river, three miles above its mouth. Another low exposure is one mile west of Montevideo on the north side of the Minnesota, halfway between the river and the bluff. Close south of Montevideo, a knob of gray gneiss, nearly vertical, with W. S. W strike, rises 30 feet above the bottom-land. One to two miles south-east from Montevideo are extensive outcrops of gneiss, rising 40 to 60 feet and extending one and a half miles from the river to the bluff at its north-east side. At a little lake near the river its dip is 45° S. 10°—20° E. Adjoining this, the gneiss includes a mass of hornblende schist, 20 rods long from north-west to south-east and from 20 feet to 6 rods wide. Its dip is 33° S. E. by S. At the railroad cut the rock is reddish gray gneiss, dipping 45° to 60° S. E. Two to four miles south-east from these outcrops are others of small extent, also on the north side of Minnesota river.

At Granite Falls and Minnesota Falls ledges of gneiss occur on both sides of the river, filling the valley with a multitude of knobs and short ridges 30 to 75 feet high. These rocks begin five miles above Granite Falls, near the mouth of Stony Run. Along this distance they occur principally on the south-west side. In the N. E. ¼ of sec. 24, Stony Run, the strike for an eighth of a mile is S. 80° E., the dip being 75° N. 10° E Generally, however, the strike is nearly N. E. to S. W., the dip being south-easterly. In the north-west edge of Granite Falls, the dip is 60° S. E., but more commonly it ranges between 25° and 40°. In a few places at Granite Falls it is toward the north-east or north. At Minnesota Falls it was noted in one place to be 58° S. 10° E., and near by 85° in the same direction. These are exceptions, while the prevailing inclination is toward the south-east. The strata are reddish or gray gneiss, frequently so disintegrated by the weather that its outcrops have become turfed, varying occasionally to more enduring gray and red granites. These rocks also sometimes include trap dikes, of massive, very heavy, dark green rock, as at the rapids, recently used for manufacturing, one mile above Granite Falls, where two dikes, respectively 20 and 48 feet wide, occur 54 feet apart, their course being N. E. to S. W., conformable with the strike of the rocks. Elsewhere the gneiss may include a bed or lenticular mass of hornblende schist, as is seen at the east end of Granite Falls bridge and dam. Gray syenite, probably valuable for building and ornamental purposes, occurs about a half mile south from Minnesota Falls. A large specimen of it, elegantly polished, was shown me by Mr. Park Worden of this place. It is composed of white quartz and black hornblende, in nearly equal parts, somewhat schistose as to the direction of its grains. The trap dikes, hornblende schist, syenite and granites, are together but a small portion of these rocks which mainly are gneiss. Its outcrops from Granite Falls to one mile below Minnesota Falls are very prominent, rising in irregular and picturesque confusion throughout the entire valley, nearly two miles wide. Lower ledges continue less frequently for a mile or two beyond these.

The next outcrops noted are six miles down the river, along its portion called Patterson's Rapids, which extend, with frequent intervals of smooth current, seven miles or more, through t. 114, r. 37. The river here divides Sacred Heart on the north from Swede's Forest on the south. In the northwest corner of Swede's Forest, ledges abound for two miles, reaching 40 to 75 feet above the river. A lone school-house is situated among them, near the north-east corner of sec. 18. Half a mile west from this, the rock is reddish gray gneiss, dipping 15° N. N. W. A third of a mile west from it, are massive granite cliffs, divided by joints into nearly square blocks, 10 to 15 feet in dimension. This rock may be found valuable for quarrying. One-eighth of a mile east from the last, it is gneiss, dipping 15° S. At the east side of the school-house, it is also gneiss, dipping about 5° S.

Along the entire river-boundary between Redwood and Renville counties, a distance of 30 miles, ledges of gneiss and granite abound, in some places enclosing masses of hornblende schist. For 12 miles above Beaver Falls they fill the whole valley, occurring on each side of the river, and rising 50 to 125 feet above it. Between Beaver and Birch Cooley creeks the outcrops are mainly on the north side of the Minnesota, rising in their highest portions 100 feet above the river. Below the mouth of Birch Cooley they are mostly on the south side, occurring in great abundance for two miles above and three miles below the mouth of Wabashaw creek. The highest of these are a mile above this creek, rising 75 to 125, or perhaps 140 feet, above the river. It will be remembered that the bluffs along all this part of the valley are about 175 feet high, so that none of these ledges was visible before the surface of the drift-sheet had been considerably channelled. At Birum's mill, on the Redwood river where it enters the Minnesota valley, 1½ miles northeast from Redwood Falls, the rock is a greenish talcose quartzyte, dipping 25° S. E. One mile north-east from this, on the opposite side of the Minnesota and one fourth of a mile north of the ford, the rock is gray gneiss, weathering to reddish gray, apparently almost vertical, with its strike E. N. E. At the east side of the road this gneiss is crossed by a nearly vertical vein, 1 to 3 feet wide, of coarsely crystalline feldspar and quartz, extending within sight 50 feet. These strata are also exposed in the valley of Beaver creek one and two miles above its junction with the Minnesota valley. The Champion mill-dam at the village of Beaver Falls is nearly within the line of strike of the gneiss described north of the ford, and a similar gneiss, with nearly the same strike, is found here. Its dip is 15° S. S. E. At the dam of the O K mill, one mile north-east from the last, is an extensive exposure of gray gneiss, also with E. N. E. strike; it is nearly vertical, or has a steep dip to the S. S. E., and in some portions is much contorted. Veins, 6 to 18 inches wide, of coarsely crystalline flesh-colored feldspar, coinciding with the strike, are common here. The valley of Birch Cooley, one mile above its entrance into that of the Minnesota, has a large exposure of granite, holding interesting veins, faulted and divided portions of which are figured in Prof. Winchell's report. One of these veins, composed of granite and four inches wide, is traceable 250 feet, running south-west.

Two miles below the mouth of Birch Cooley, a low outcrop examined on the north side of the river is granite, containing a large proportion of flesh-colored feldspar. Ledges were next seen on the north side three miles below the last, in the vicinity of the line between Birch Cooley and Camp, extending a half mile westward from Reikie and Fenske's flour mill. A small outcrop occurs five miles south-east from these, beside a small round lakelet in the bottom-land north of the river. One mile farther south-east, in the west extremity of Ridgely township, and 1½ miles west of Fort Ridgely, are the ledges which supplied the stone used in building the fort. An excavation found near the north end of the outcrop, is in porphyritic granite, which contains abundant gray feldspar crystals, ¾ to 1½ inches long and one third to two thirds as wide; it also contains occasional masses six to twelve inches long and half as wide, mostly made up of black mica in small grains. This ledge is also traversed by several flesh-colored feldspathic veins, 2 to 6 inches wide. The other rock-masses near by are mostly feldspathic granite, flesh-colored, not noticeably porphyritic. In one band here, the rock is hornblende schist and mica schist, much contorted, weathering to a very rough honey-combed surface. This band extends several rods from north to south, and dips 45° to 60° W.

Four miles below Fort Ridgely, at Little Rock creek, which is a mere rill, ledges again appear. They extend one mile from north-west to south-east, lying on the north side of the river, and rising 40 to 60 feet above it. This rock is partly gneiss, much contorted and often obscure in its lamination, and partly granite, both being flesh-colored, apparently from weathering. It is abundantly jointed and seamed. The dip is not clearly exhibited. Prof. Winchell thought, from the outlines and slopes of surface, that it might be 35° or 40° to the north.

Thirteen miles of the valley next to the south-east have no rock exposures. Two small outcrops of granite follow this, lying in the bottom-land of the S. W. ¼ of sec. 27, Courtland. It is a coarse granite, the greater part of it consisting of flesh-colored feldspar. Weathering has made it very friable on the surface, but the interior is solid. This is the last occurrence of the rocks of this series seen in the Minnesota valley. It is about 300 feet west from the south end of a conglomerate outcrop, and one mile northwest from the quartzyte at Redstone.

Examination of these notes as to strike and dip shows that the axial lines of folds in these rocks run mainly from north-east to south-west. Very thorough detailed exploration would be requisite, but very probably, being confined to this narrow valley, would be insufficient to determine the position of synclinal, anticlinal and inverted axes, or to arrive at any stratigraphic divisions of the series. No quarrying of any importance has been yet undertaken in any portion of these rocks in the Minnesota valley; but they are extensively quarried at St. Cloud, both for building and monumental stone.

Wells in Metamorphic Rocks. A well drilled for the railroad, at Herman, Grant county, passed through 124 feet of till, and then went 65 feet in rock. The first seven or eight feet of the rock was the fine grained, buff, magnesian limestone, boulders of which are common throughout northwestern Minnesota. Prof. Winchell thinks it probable that this portion was a compacted mass of boulders. This seems to be the rock which Owen observed in the bank of the Red river above Fergus Falls. His statement shows that possibly it was there only a large slab, embedded in nearly horizontal position in the bank, instead of being in place as a solid bed. This rock outcrops in the vicinity of Winnipeg, in Manitoba. The remaining 57 feet drilled in the rock was through quartzose granite, with red feldspar; white micaceous quartzyte; and mica schist of several varieties.

The section of the salt-well at Belle Plaine was as follows, in descending order: 216 feet of stratified gravels, sands, and clays, all apparently belonging to the glacial period; 16 feet of sandstone; 10 feet of ochreous shale; 176 feet of highly magnesian clays, purple and speckled with white, mostly without siliceous grains; and 292 feet of siliceous, unctuous shale, highly ferruginous, sometimes amygdaloidal, and varying to a micaceous quartzyte. From 216 to 418 feet, the strata are thought to represent the quartzyte and pipestone of Potsdam age, which outcrop near New Ulm and in Pipestone county; from 418 feet to the bottom of the well at 710, they are considered lower than the Potsdam sandstone; but the granites and gneisses lie yet deeper. No other wells in the district here reported penetrate to the metamorphic rocks.

Decomposed Gneiss and Granite. Very remarkable chemical changes have taken place in the upper portions of many of the exposures of gneiss and granite near Redwood Falls. The rock is transformed to a soft, earthy or clayey mass, resembling kaolin. It has a blue or greenish color, when freshly exposed; but when weathered, assumes a yellowish ash color, and finally becomes white and glistening. Mica scales and laminæ of quartz are generally contained in this material, and have the same arrangement as in gneiss, so that the dip can be distinctly seen. Veins of quartz or feldspar, the latter completely decomposed, and the lines of joints, are also noticeable, just as in granite or gneiss; making it evident that this substance is the result of a decay of the rocks in their original place. So far as can be judged from stream channels and other exposures, this decomposition reaches in some places to a depth of 20 or 30 feet, perhaps more. All grades of change may be found, from ledges where only here and there a few spots have been attacked and slightly decomposed, to portions where nearly every indication of its origin has been obliterated.

Before the extensive denudation of the glacial period, it is probable that all the granite and gneiss of this region were covered by a similarly decayed surface. Upon the areas where decomposed rocks still exist, the glacial ploughing was shallower than elsewhere. These beds are frequently overlain by Cretaceous deposits, and appear to have been submerged beneath a Cretaceous ocean. Prof. Winchell suggests that their decay may have taken place during this submergence, under the influence of the abundance of alkaline chemical agents held in solution by the sea in that age. Exposures of these kaolinized strata are found in a ravine north of the river opposite Minnesota Falls; in the gorge of Redwood river below Redwood Falls, interesting for its grand and beautiful scenery; in many of the ledges of Minnesota valley for several miles next below, especially in exposures made by roads at the foot of the bluffs; in the valley of Birch Cooley near its mouth; and occasionally for 8 or 10 miles farther down the valley.

The Conglomerate opposite New Ulm. This outcrop is about 1000 feet long, in which distance its height rises from 10 to about 60 feet above the river. Its strike or course is N. 20° E., while the dip, measured by Prof. Winchell, is 18° E. S. E. Its greatest exposure vertically at any one place is about 20 feet. The beds vary from 1 to 6 feet in thickness. It is a massive, tough conglomerate. The pebbles in it are all more or less water-worn; they are generally abundant, often occurring nearly as thick as they could be packed. They are of all sizes up to a diameter of one foot or a little more. These pebbles are remarkable as consisting, almost without exception, of only two kinds of rock, which occur together in nearly equal abundance and dimensions. One of the two classes is apparently a jasper, usually dull red and massive, but in many of the fragments laminated, or in thin bands, which are sometimes dark, sometimes yellow; the other class is white quartz, massive, now and then containing foreign particles, and occasionally smoky in color. The origin of this conglomerate may have been from the action of sea-waves upon a coast where only these two kinds of rock were exposed. The only pebble found, which could not be referred to these classes, was a scrap of fine-grained gneiss, two inches long. Neither the granite that outcrops close at the west, nor the quartzyte that occurs upon a large area at a mile to the east, seems to be represented. The conglomerate is probably older than the quartzyte, but both are thought to come within the Potsdam epoch.

The Quartzyte at Redstone. This lies on the north-east side of the river, beginning at the Redstone railroad-bridge, and extending one mile to the east and south-east. The highest knobs of its southern part rise 100 to 125 feet above the river, while its most northern part forms a nearly level tract of about equal height, ¾ of a mile long, lying at the south side of the carriage road. The greater part of this outcrop dips northerly. South of the west railroad-cut the dip is 27° N. 10° E. At another cut, a third of a mile east from this, it is 45° N. N. E. It frequently varies as much as 10° within a few rods, and its north portion seems to be nearly level in stratification. The thickness exposed in the whole outcrop may be 250 feet. The rock is a compact hard quartzyte, of red or reddish gray color. It is variously divided by joints, and its solid masses often have a tendency to break into rhomboidal fragments. The layers are 3 to 12 inches thick, mostly without lamination at the north; but at the south-west they show fine laminæ, part of which are shale softer than the rest of the rock. At the north-west it rarely encloses small pebbles, the largest seen being three-quarters of an inch in diameter. They include only red jasper and white quartz, like those of the conglomerate just described. Stone suitable for cellar-walls and foundations is quarried from this formation.

St. Lawrence Limestone. Eleven miles south-east from the quartzyte, we find at Hebron and Judson the first exposure of the Lower Magnesian rocks within the Minnesota valley. Thence to the limit of our survey at Hamilton these rocks occur frequently. They consist of three members, named in ascending order the St. Lawrence limestone, Jordan sandstone and Shakopee limestone, from the lowest places in this valley at which they are well exposed.

The St. Lawrence limestone at Hebron extends from Nicollet creek, the outlet of Swan lake, about 1½ miles eastward It rises 25 to 35 feet above the river, against which it forms a barrier, protecting a broad terrace of modified drift that lies between the limestone exposures and the foot of the bluffs. Its stratification is nearly level, the dip being about 2° to the southeast. The beds are 1 to 4 inches thick at top, where it has been affected by weathering; below they are 4 to 12 inches thick. The rock is a fine-grained compact magnesian limestone, yellowish or reddish gray, often streaked or speckled with green. Its layers are generally separated by a thin film, or sometimes by a seam ½ inch thick, of dark green crumbling sandstone. The upper part of these beds in the race-way of the Hebron stone-mill contains a layer of soft sandstone one foot thick. Several quarries are worked slightly on each side of the river.

Other exposures of this limestone in the Minnesota valley are few. It is next recognized in two low outcrops, a mile apart, at the east side of Sibley county, 30 miles from Hebron in a straight line. The first is on land of Henry Young, in the south part of sec. 13, Jessenland. The rock is yellowish buff limestone, nearly level in stratification, in layers 1 to 4 inches thick, much divided and broken by vertical and oblique seams and cracks. A half dozen kilns of lime have been burned from this rock within the past two years. The second outcrop is owned by Walter E. Doheny, and lies in the south-west corner of Faxon, only a short distance from the town line and river. Its extent, height, stratification, and jointed condition are nearly the same as in the last. It is a dull red, slightly arenaceous limestone. A quarry seven feet deep shows layers 1 to 5 inches thick, often separated by thin earthy seams.

In St. Lawrence, 10 miles north-east from the foregoing, this limestone occurs occasionally for a distance of nearly two miles, having its top about 45 feet above the river. It is nearly level in stratification, in beds from 2 to 18 inches thick. The color is buff, reddish, or yellowish gray, usually with frequent green specks. In composition it is a siliceous magnesian limestone. It has been considerably quarried, and supplies good building stone. A vertical thickness of about 15 feet is seen in quarries and natural exposures; and wells here have drilled into it 24 feet, without reaching its base.

The reference of all these outcrops to a horizon below the Jordan sandstone is based on their lithological character, and on the position and stratification of neighboring rocks belonging higher in this group. At Jordan, 3 miles east from St. Lawrence, wells encounter the St. Lawrence limestone, pinkish buff in color and very compact and hard, lying directly beneath the soft and friable Jordan sandstone. At the upper brewery the well was 12 feet deep, 10 feet in sandstone and 2 feet in limestone. The well of the lower brewery, 11 feet deep, was dug 6 feet in sandstone, and then 5 feet in this very hard limestone. Below this it was drilled 25 feet, all the way in limestone, which was thought to grow harder; its base was not reached. The limestone also occurs in the bed of Sand creek, at the pier of the private bridge in front of the lower brewery. All these exposures of St. Lawrence limestone in the Minnesota valley probably exhibit its upper portion, and its thickness here remains undetermined. In Fillmore and Houston counties it is about 200 feet thick, forming more than half of the Lower Magnesian group.

The Jordan Sandstone. Next above the last is a coarse-grained sandstone; white or light gray, or often somewhat stained with iron-rust. It is usually soft and crumbling, so that it is readily excavated with a shovel; but some of its beds, quarried at Jordan, yield stone sufficiently durable for the construction of large mills and bridge masonry. It becomes harder upon exposure to the air, and its ledges sometimes have an indurated surface while they are quite friable within. The stratification is level or nearly so, in beds that vary from six inches to 3 feet in thickness. While each of these layers is plainly horizontal, its lamination is frequently oblique, being inclined 5° to 20°. This structure is the same with that often seen in recent sand-deposits, where the material was spread and arranged by strong currents. The direction of this inclination is variable, and seems to indicate the action of tides or waves in water of no great depth. This sandstone, however, extends over a large area, with a comparatively uniform thickness, which is 40 or 50 feet in the Minnesota valley and 25 to 40 feet in Fillmore and Houston counties.

In the vicinity of Mankato this sandstone underlies the Shakopee limestone at the quarries upon each side of the river. They also occur in the same manner, forming bluffs, at Kasota, St. Peter, Ottawa and Louisville, as will be more fully described in speaking of the limestone.

Very extensive exposures of the Jordan sandstone are seen beside the river-road in Oshawa, extending 3 miles above St. Peter. It is easily disintegrated, which often causes slightly harder layers near the top to overhang. Many excavations, used for the same purpose as cellars, have been made in these cliffs. This sandstone also forms the foot of the bluffs at the south side of a creek that enters the Minnesota at the north-east corner of Traverse township. At these places the sandstone rises 40 or 50 feet above the river, and is capped by Shakopee limestone, less conspicuously exposed.

In Lake Prairie the sandstone is seen at several places, as in a ravine crossed by the river-road nearly opposite Ottawa, and at Patrick Osborn's and Frank Linter's, within 1½ miles farther north. Its top in all these localities is about 35 feet above the river; and at Mr. Osborn's the Shakopee limestone is seen overlying it. At and near Mr. Linter's the sandstone forms three outcrops, not protected by its usual cap of limestone. The well here went through soil and drift, 5 feet; gray and white sandstone, 25 feet, sand, 10 feet, an unconsolidated layer of this stone; and white sandstone, as above, 10 feet. Water comes at the bottom, which is probably near the underlying limestone.

At Jordan this sandstone forms numerous outcrops for three-fourths of a mile along the valley of Sand creek. The St. Lawrence limestone is found beneath it here, as already described. The stratification at this place is horizontal, and the exposures are between 35 and 75 feet, approximately, above the river. Here and in several outcrops of this rock occurring within 6 miles northward in the Minnesota valley, the overlying Shakopee limestone is wanting. Four miles from Jordan, in the south edge of Louisville, are extensive exposures of the sandstone, rising about 40 feet above the river.

At the highway bridge over Van Oser's creek, these beds dip 15° W. N. W., owing to some local disturbance which does not generally affect this area. Little Rapids in the Minnesota river, one and a half miles to the west, is caused by two nearly level outcrops of this sandstone.

The Shakopee Limestone. This highest member of the Lower Magnesian group is seen at many places overlying the stratum last described. It is a magnesian limestone of buff color, often mottled in alternate red and yellow tints. The stratification is nearly level in beds from a few inches to three feet or more in thickness. In some places, as at Kasota, in the Asylum quarry at St. Peter, and at Mankato, a part of these beds are compact and supply an excellent stone for every purpose in building or monumental work ; but generally this rock is much broken by little hollows and crevices, and is of unequal texture, some portions being especially sandy or coarse in grain, or having contorted and obscure lamination. It is burned extensively for lime at Mankato, Caroline station, Ottawa, Louisville and Shakopee. The only observation of any rock lying upon this limestone in the Minnesota valley is at the Asylum quarry, where Prof. Winchell found it covered by two feet of white friable sandstone, with a thin strip of green shale about midway in it. This is supposed to be the St. Peter sandstone, which is known to be next in stratigraphic order above this limestone ; it may, however, be a Cretaceous deposit. The Shakopee limestone in the Minnesota valley varies in thickness from about 50 feet thus indicated here to 70 or 80 feet at Shakopee ; in Fillmore county it is about 75 feet ; in Wilmington, Houston county, it has been found to be 64 feet.

In Belgrade, opposite Mankato, about 40 feet of Shakopee limestone are exposed, affording valuable quarries. In a ravine about 25 rods west of the principal quarry here, the underlying Jordan sandstone is seen for 7 feet vertically, its top being about 30 feet above the river. At the quarries in the north part of Mankato, 50 feet of limestone is shown resting upon the Jordan sandstone at about 25 feet above the river. A terrace of these strata, averaging a mile in width and 75 feet in height above the river, extends thence 7 miles northward to Kasota ; beyond which it is continued in decreasing height on the other side of the river through St. Peter. The railroad well at Kasota station went through drift, mostly limestone gravel, 8 feet ; solid limestone, 21 feet ; and sandstone, 6 feet. Here and generally in this vicinity, the base of the limestone is about 40 feet above the river ; but it sinks to about half this height in going 1½ miles northward in St. Peter, between the railroad-bridge and the highway-bridge.

Ottawa is situated on another terrace of Shakopee limestone underlain by Jordan sandstone. Their junction in the bluff near Charles Schwartz' lime-kiln, called White Rock bluff by Dr. Shumard, is about 45 feet above the river. The terrace generally rises 20 or 25 feet higher, which is probably the average depth of the limestone remaining here.

The next extensive exposures of the Shakopee limestone are found in Louisville, 30 miles farther down the valley. Quarries which supply good stone for foundations and bridge masonry are worked here on land of Mrs. M. A. Spencer, 1½ miles south-east from Carver. Here the limestone has a thickness of about 30 feet, and 4 feet of the Jordan sandstone is visible below it, their junction being at 12 or 15 feet above the river. This is the lowest point in the valley at which the Jordan sandstone has been seen. A terrace of this limestone, 40 to 50 feet above the*river, extends thence two miles northward. The St. Paul & Sioux City railroad is built upon this; and · close at its east side another terrace, formed by the upper part of this limestone, rises 40 feet higher. A quarry in its top half supplies rock for lime-burning at a point a half mile east from the Spencer quarry. A level-topped outlier of the upper terrace occurs 50 rods south-west from these lime-kilns.

At Shakopee the limestone rises from the river's edge to a height of 50 feet, its upper 20 feet being quarried for lime. Beneath the terrace of sand and gravel at the south and south-east, commonly called " Shakopee prairie," the limestone is found at a depth of 40 or 50 feet, its top being 60 to 70 feet above the river. Water is obtained in the wells on this terrace only after drilling 60 to 80 feet in the limestone. Thus Major H. B. Strait's well, 122 feet deep, is soil and sand, 8 feet; clay, 30; limestone, 84, its last 5 feet being light gray in color; water abundant, rising 9 feet. J. A. Wilder's well, 112 feet deep, is soil, 2; yellow stratified clay, 5; sand and gravel, inter-stratified, coarsest below, 38; hard limestone, 61; quicksand and sandstone, 2 feet, containing plenty of water, which does not rise; "flint rocks," 4 feet. These are within the incorporated limits of Shakopee. Amos Riggs' well,. 1½ miles south-east from these, in the S. E. ¼ of sec. 18, Eagle Creek, is 115 feet deep, in order as follows: soil, 2; sand and fine gravel, 38; very coarse gravel, with pebbles up to 1½ feet in diameter, 10 feet; rotten sandy limestone, picked, 5 feet; limestone drilled, nearly all alike, 60; water comes abundantly at 107, not rising.

Four miles east of Shakopee, on land of Thomas Durose, sec. 3, Eagle Creek, this limestone has a low outcrop near the river, which has been slightly quarried. About six miles farther east, at Hamilton, is the lowest point at which the Shakopee limestone is seen in the Minnesota valley. Here it occurs for about 50 feet along the bottom of the raceway of Quinn Brothers' mill, at a height of 20 or 25 feet above the river. Farther east this limestone sinks below the level of the river, and the bluffs of Fort Snelling and its vicinity are composed of the overlying St. Peter sandstone capped by Trenton limestone.

It is interesting to note the nearly level position of these very ancient. strata, which have scarcely suffered any disturbance since their deposition. Alternately beds of limestone and sandstone were accumulated upon the floor of the Paleozoic sea, and they have been lifted 600 to 1000 feet or more without being broken or tilted. The height above sea of the base of the Shakopee limestone where it has been observed within the Minnesota valley,. is at Mankato, 760 to 795; at Kasota, about 785; at St. Peter bridge, about 760; at Ottawa, 780; and at Louisville, about 720. The distance included is 45 miles in a straight line.

The Lower Magnesian group in this valley is nearly destitute of fossils. In the Shakopee limestone, Prof. Winchell found *Orthis* at Mr. Clapp's quarry for lime-burning in the S. E. ¼ of sec. 17, Kasota; and Dr. Shumard found *Lingula Dakotaensis* and trilobite fragments at Kasota, and the same, with another species of *Lingula* and an *Orthis*, at the White Rock or Ottawa bluff. In the Jordan sandstone, Dr. Shumard found *Straparollus Minnesotensis* a mile above Traverse des Sioux and again at Kasota.

The Cretaceous. The first important exposures of Cretaceous beds found in descending the Minnesota river, are in the valley cut by the Redwood river below Redwood Falls, where a lignitic bed of clay or shale has been explored by a drift to the distance of 40 feet. This bed varies from 7 to 2½ feet in thickness. It is a nearly black, more or less clayey deposit, and contains much lignite of two kinds, one pulverized or in small fragments, resembling charcoal, the other hard and compact, in larger lumps, appearing like cannel coal. In the bank of Crow creek, 3½ miles below Redwood Falls, beds of the same character, 4 feet or more in thickness, and containing leaf impressions, have been explored by drifting some 200 feet. They also occur and have been somewhat tested in several other ravines in that vicinity. A similar coaly layer, 1½ feet thick, has been tunnelled into 40 feet upon the east side of Fort creek, a third of a mile east of Fort Ridgely. No compact, continuous seam of coal has been yet found in any of these beds, though much search has been made. The fragments obtained are insufficient in amount to be of any practical value. They are the same with the pieces of "charcoal" and "stone coal" that are sparingly scattered in the drift throughout all south-western Minnesota, so that frequently one or two are found in digging a well. The origin of these pieces, which vary in size up to 3 or very rarely 6 inches in diameter, is from beds like the foregoing that have been ploughed up by the ice-sheet. It appears nearly certain that no workable coal deposits exist in this region.

Sandy marl, horizontally stratified, probably Cretaceous, is seen in the lower part of the bluff below the Lower Sioux Agency, three miles south-east from Crow creek. Two miles farther east, on the north side of the river, concretionary marl or limy earth, nearly white, occurs in the banks of a small creek about three-quarters of a mile from its entrance into the Minnesota valley. An overlying bed of similar material, colored and hardened by iron-rust, is exposed 18 feet vertically.

In New Ulm the grading of Third North street close north-east of the railroad, exposes Cretaceous clays. This cut is 14 feet deep and 200 feet long. Its upper 4 feet are soil and drift, containing and overspread with many boulders of granite, gneiss and schists, up to 6 feet in diameter. The remaining 10 feet are curved, contorted, and irregularly interstratified, red, yellow, green and gray clays. They are free from gravel, but contain flat, limy concretions, in some portions abundant up to one inch in diameter, and elsewhere joined in sheets a foot or less in length and a half inch or less in thickness, conforming with the stratification. These strata are eroded and covered unconformably by the drift. The terraces on which New Ulm is built have a surface of drift, mostly stratified gravel and sand, 10 to 20 feet thick ; underlain by beds that are probably of Cretaceous age, consisting of fine blue clay, bedded, weathering white, 4 to 10 feet thick, and sand or fine gravel, readily crumbling and containing rounded lumps of a fine white powder, exposed 20 to 30 feet vertically. Deposits of clay, which have been much used for the manufacture of fire-bricks and pottery, occur in the banks of the Waraju or Big Cottonwood river south-west of New Ulm. These with associated sandy marl, sandstone, and thick beds of sand, are probably Cretaceous deposits. Other beds of this period, consisting of cavernous and nodular gray limestone, much of which has been burned for lime, interstratified with green and red clay and shale, occur on the north side of the river about a mile below New Ulm, being half way between the conglomerate and quartzyte, and again a mile farther south-east on the south side. In each place these strata form a terrace about 35 feet above the river.

Eight miles below New Ulm on the north side of the river, Cretaceous sandstone has been slightly quarried on land of William Fritz, in the N. E. ¼ of sec. 16, Courtland. It lies in layers from 1 to 6 feet thick, some of which contain fragments of wood, charcoal, and angiospermous leaves. Interstratified with these layers are others, 6 inches to 3 feet thick, of white uncemented sand. Several outcrops are found here and others appear occasionally for a mile south-eastward, varying in height from 25 to 40 feet above the river. The same rock occurs again on land of Henry Greenholtz, 3 miles south-east from the last, in sec. 24, Courtland, and has been quarried a little for culverts and cellar-walls. Its outcrop is 30 rods south-east from his house, and about 35 feet above the river. There is an irregular slope at each of these localities, amounting to about 50 feet in ¼ mile or less, between the foot of the bluffs and the river.

All the strata here described and referred to the Cretaceous age, lie in a nearly horizontal position beneath the drift. They have only yielded fossils in a few places, and these have been mostly obscure plant remains and lignite. Similar formations, containing characteristic Cretaceous fossils, have a great development in the region drained by the upper Missouri river.

The Shakopee limestone at Mankato, St. Peter, and Ottawa, contains in its cavities and fissures singular deposits of greenish or bluish clay, which becomes white by exposure to the weather. At the railroad bridge across the Blue Earth river, a cut in this limestone shows hollows and crevices reaching 20 feet below the top of the rock. These cavities are water-worn, and their surface is thinly covered by iron ore, from a half inch to an inch and a half thick. Within them, after this ferruginous crust was formed, clay has been sifted and packed so as to fill irregular spaces, often several feet in diameter, enclosed and partially covered by the limestone. The clay here is greenish or bluish, weathering white, in some portions sandy, horizontally bedded, or conforming somewhat to the shape of the hollow that holds it. The quarries at St. Peter contain in clefts and water-worn cavities a similar greenish white silt, holding much sand and many angular flinty fragments. At Ottawa, John R. Clark's quarry exposes a nearly vertical seam of this clay, 1 to 2 feet wide, 6 feet deep and extending lower, seen here for 8 rods in a nearly west-to-east course. Nearly in the line of its continuation, at 25 rods farther east, the same clay was found in Charles Needham's well, in a similar seam, reaching down 15 feet in the limestone. At St. Peter and Ottawa no marks of stratification can be seen. None of these clays have yielded any fossils. Their probable origin has been shown by Prof. Winchell, who attributes them to deposition while this region was deeply covered by the Cretaceous ocean.

Glacial Drift. The presence at many points in the Minnesota valley of decomposed granite and gneiss, and of Cretaceous beds, both of which would yield readily to eroding agencies, shows that the moving ice-sheet did not everywhere plough up all the loose material under it. A considerable depth, however, has probably been removed; and these may be scanty remnants of thick beds which covered this region generally before the glacial period. More commonly the ice-sheet removed all such material, and gathered a part of its drift from the underlying solid rocks; as is shown by their being frequently rounded, smoothed, and marked with parallel furrows and scratches, called striæ. Similarly scratched pebbles and boulders are found in the glacial drift. These were the graving tools by which the bed-rock was worn and striated. They were held firmly by being frozen in the bottom of the ice and were pushed forward by its current, which thus recorded its direction. Our observations of striæ are of course limited to the rock exposures seen along the Minnesota valley, and there many of the rocks are so disintegrated by the weather that these marks are effaced.

Courses of Striæ in the Valley of the Minnesota River,
referred to the true meridian.

Locality.	Formation.	Course.
1 to 3 miles S. E. from foot of Big Stone lake,	......Granite, ...	..S. E.
F. Frankhaus', S. E. ¼ of sec. 32. t. 121, r. 45,	......Granite, ...	..S. E.
S. E. part of Granite Falls, on N. E. side of river, at several places,	........Gneiss,......	..S. 45° -50° E.
Beaver Falls, at dam of O K mill,	.......Gneiss,......	..S. 60° E.
2 miles below Birch Cooley creek, N. W. ¼ of sec. 10, t. 112, r. 34,	......Granite,......	..S. 60° E.
1½ miles west from Fort Ridgely,	......Granite,......	..S. 60° E.
Redstone, 1½ miles S. E. from New Ulm,	.....Quartzyte,....	..S. 25° E. ·
Jordan, observed at several places by Foss, Wells & Co., in quarrying and on site of their mill	Jordan Sandstone,	..S. E.

In the topographic description of this region it has been pointed out that this valley lies nearly midway between parallel terminal moraines, which extend from north-west to south-east, about 80 miles apart; that on the north-east reaching from the Leaf hills to Glenwood, Minnetonka lake, and Rice county, and that on the south-west being the well-known massive Coteau des Prairies. These series of drift-hills are connected by a loop that passes through Hancock, Kossuth and Palo Alto counties in northern Iowa, making a single contemporaneous series shaped like the letter **U**, and bounding the area covered by a vast lobe or tongue of the ice-sheet. Near the center of this area the glacial current, as shown by these striæ, was in the direction of its axis or south-easterly; but in approaching its margin we must suppose that it was everywhere deflected to a course nearly perpendicular to its terminal moraine. The straight trunk and divergent branches of a tree may illustrate our idea of the axial and marginal motions of the ice-fields upon this area. The terminal moraine accumulated at their border has been described under the head of topography, so far as it has yet been explored.

The most remarkable features of our glacial deposits are their great depth and extent. It has been already stated that the old rocks are almost everywhere concealed; nor are they reached by the deepest wells, which go down 75 to 250 feet without passing through the drift, except in two or three instances, upon this entire area of 16,000 square miles. Through all this part of the State the drift probably averages as deep as along the course of

Minnesota river, where a channel cut down in many places to the older rocks shows these superficial deposits to be from 100 to 200 feet thick. We are not yet able to estimate what portion of this material was here before the glacial period, in the form of decomposed and in part solid rock, Cretaceous strata, mostly unconsolidated, and the alluvium of rivers. The aggregate of these was great, but it seems probable that this thick drift-sheet includes in addition to these materials an equally large amount brought by the ice-current from areas farther north.

Till, or unmodified glacial drift, known also as hardpan or boulder-clay, consisting of clay, sand, gravel, and boulders, mixed indiscriminately together, makes up nearly the whole of this great mass of superficial deposits ; excepting the lacustrine plain of the Red River valley, filled by Lake Agassiz during the retreat of the ice-sheet, and the east part of Becker and Otter Tail counties, which are mainly modified drift. Very finely pulverized rock, forming a stiff, compact, unctuous clay, is the principal ingredient of the till upon this area, whether at great depths or at the surface. The admixture of sand and gravel is somewhat variable, being often greater in the upper than in the lower part of the till. It is rarely enough to cause the side of a well or cellar to fall down at the time of excavation. Layers of sand and gravel are frequently enclosed in the till. They are commonly from a few inches to a few feet in thickness, and often are filled with water. At considerable depths the water is generally under hydrostatic pressure, which causes it to rise in wells to within 10, 20 or 30 feet below the surface, sometimes even overflowing. Thick beds of stratified gravel, sand and clay, varying from 10 to 50 or 75 feet, also occur occasionally below till, which is again found beneath them where these stratified deposits have been penetrated.

The till is also found, even where not so divided by intercalations of modified drift, to be in massive beds which differ from each other as to color, hardness, and relative proportions of clay, sand, and stones, these changes being often noticed together at a definite line. The most notable distinction in color is that the upper part of the till, to a depth that varies from 5 to 50 feet, but is most commonly between 10 and 30 feet, is yellowish, due to the influence of air and water upon the iron contained in this deposit, changing it from the protoxide state to hydrated sesquioxide. At greater depths the color is much darker and usually bluish. In a few instances a yellow bed of till is reported beneath or enclosed in the blue till. Several observations show that the yellow color of the till, in its upper portion, has been mainly produced by exposure to the weather since its formation, and was not probably occasioned by differences in the conditions of its accumulation in and beneath the ice-sheet.

Another important difference in the till is that its upper portion is more commonly softer and easily dug with a shovel, while below there is a sudden change to a hard and compact deposit, which must be picked and is often three times as expensive for excavation. There is frequently a thin layer of sand or gravel between these kinds of till, which have their division line at a depth that varies from 5 to 30 or very rarely 40 feet. Owing to the more compact and impervious character of the lower till, the change to a yellow color is usually limited to the upper till. There are instances, however, where this weathering has not reached to the line that divides the softer from the harder till, and others where it has extended considerably lower. The probable cause of this difference in hardness was the pressure of the vast weight of the ice-sheet upon the lower till, while the upper till was contained in the ice and dropped loosely at its melting.

Again, in numerous places the upper till as here described is directly underlain by a softer till, moist and sticky, and dark bluish in color. This is usually of considerable thickness, or between 20 and 50 feet. It often encloses or is underlain by beds of water-bearing sand ; but occasionally it has been penetrated and is found to lie directly upon a bed of very compact till, such as usually comes next below the upper till. In some cases this soft and moist deposit is evidently stratified clay, free from gravel or only holding here and there a stone, and all varieties appear to be found between this and an unstratified and very pebbly till ; as indeed it may be that the latter in different localities shows all gradations from its occasionally very soft character, where a shovel can be easily thrust into it to the depth of a foot or more, to the hardest deposits of the lower till in which a pick can be driven only an inch or two at one blow.

The few beds found in this district which contain shells or trees that flourished in interglacial epochs, lie beneath two distinct beds of till, the lower sometimes showing its usual hard and compact character, but elsewhere being even softer than the upper till.

Excepting the division into beds as before described, the till is an entirely unstratified deposit. There has been no assortment by water of its materials, and the coarsest and finest are mingled confusedly in the same mass. Often a thickness of fifty feet or more exhibits no evidence of stratification.

Small rock-fragments, varying in size up to the dimension of six inches, are usually numerous and scattered through all parts of the till ; they are, however, seldom abundant, and are sometimes so few that in well-boring none might be encountered. Boulders of larger size are less frequent, and often a well or even a railroad cut in till fails to display any of greater diameter than 2 or 3 feet. Again several may be found of various sizes up to 5 or perhaps 7 or 8 feet. They appear to be usually more numerous in the upper part of the till than below. The number of boulders over one foot in size to be found generally upon the surface varies from one or two to ten on an acre ; but often they are more scarce, so that perhaps a dozen could not be gathered on a square mile. Terminal and medial moraines usually contain both small and large boulders somewhat more abundantly, and very rarely they are so plentiful as to cover half the ground ; their greater numbers being the most important difference between the till forming the morainic hills and that spread in gently undulating or nearly level tracts.

The largest boulder seen in the first seven weeks of my exploration for this survey was on the hills of Langhei, the highest in Pope county. It measured 12 by 9 feet, and rose 3 feet above the surface, probably having an equal amount buried. This was the only boulder seen during this time that exceeded eight feet in diameter, though the area traversed was almost entirely till and included the Leaf hills and the continuation of this moraine for 100 miles thence to the south and south-east. Larger blocks than the foregoing were seen only in the valley of the Minnesota river, the most notable being in Big Stone county, where two boulders, about 30 and about 20 feet in diameter, lie near the railroad between Correll and Odessa stations. Nearly all the large boulders throughout this whole region are granite or gneiss, with occasionally one of some crystalline schist or of magnesian limestone.

The thick and almost universal mantle of drift prevents a reference of the varieties of these rocks to their sources. In general, the great representation of metamorphic rocks indicates that these probably occupy the greater part of this area, extending in a wide belt from the Minnesota river to their large tract in the north-east part of the State. The limestone, belonging to a period later than that of the St. Lawrence and Shakopee limestones, quite probably occurs in place beneath the drift in the north-west part of the region here reported, as is indicated by the well already mentioned at Herman, by Owen's note of limestone on the Red river above Fergus Falls, and by the great abundance and large size of its boulders at localities near Audubon and White Earth Agency in Becker county. Northward it outcrops near Winnipeg, and many of its boulders in our drift may have been carried this distance of 200 miles or more in the ice-sheet. The proportion of limestone through the north-west part of our district averages one-tenth or less of boulders exceeding a foot in diameter, while of small pebbles it often constitutes half in bulk and more than half in number. Handfuls of pebbles taken from stratified drift at Hawley, in Clay county, showed 125 of limestone, with 70 of granites and schists; at Muskoda, they were 44 and 36; five miles north of Breckenridge, two-thirds of the pebbles in a gravel bank beside the Red river are limestone. South-eastward a less proportion of limestone is generally found, and its abundance as boulders or pebbles seems to be confined to occasional areas a few miles or less in extent.

Records of wells, noting the order, thickness, and character of the various strata passed through, have been gathered in every part of the region here reported. The total number of wells thus noted is 582. Of these 97 are in localities which showed only modified drift; about an equal number left off in the upper till, or in beds of modified drift lying below it, without going deep enough to reach the lower till; about 30 were recorded because of their sudden rise of water, or for some other reason, without obtaining any particulars as to the material penetrated; and a few were in the rock-formations of the Minnesota valley; leaving 354 wells that show both the yellow and blue tills, in which the depth of the change of color, the occurrence of intercalated layers of modified drift, and generally the relative hardness of the upper and lower tills were noted. Of the last class, 182, or more than half, found the lower till notably harder than the upper till; and of this number, 53 had a layer of sand or gravel between these beds of boulder-clay. The yellow color is almost always limited by the line or stratified beds between these tills; and where the stratified drift is wanting, a sudden and well-marked change is noticed in hardness, color, and often in material.

Soft and moist, dark bluish till, stony and unstratified, underlies the upper till in 45 instances, in 9 of them being separated from the upper till by sand and gravel from 2 inches to 4 feet thick. Two of these beds of lower till had their first few feet hard and were soft below. In 21 other instances there were found beds of more or less plainly stratified, soft, dark bluish clay, which sometimes was free from all pebbles, and elsewhere was quite pebbly, or, though generally free from gravel, yet contained rarely stones of various sizes up to one foot in diameter. Of these 12 lay directly below the upper till, and 9 were below both this bed and another of hard and compact lower till. The thickness of these beds of till or of stratified clay varies from 5 to 65 feet; in 30 cases it exceeded 25 feet.

The average thickness of the upper till in 256 wells where it is underlain by much harder lower till, or by beds of modified drift, is 17 feet. The extremes are 3 to 5 feet and 40 feet. Examples were found where both the thinnest and thickest of its beds were underlain here by modified drift and there by typical lower till. About a quarter part of the deep wells in till found no noticeable difference between its upper and lower portions except that of color.

Water-bearing gravel and sand, lying in a nearly horizontal layer from a few inches to five feet in thickness, were found in 148 instances at depths in the lower till varying from 30 to 265 feet. The water almost always rises from these beds, sometimes very suddenly and with much force. At Audubon, in Becker county, water was struck at 60 feet, after boring through compact till, and its pressure was so great that it instantly threw up the auger and shafting, weighing 600 pounds, twenty feet, filling the boring with gravel to that height. In three minutes it rose and stood at two feet below the surface. Two wells in Hamden, a few miles to the north, about 75 and 100 feet deep, find water at the bottom which rises and permanently overflows. Other flowing wells are found in Wilkin, Traverse, Grant, Douglas and Chippewa counties. The deepest well found is that bored for the railroad at Stewart, in McLeod county, where the water rises from a depth of 265 feet and stands at 5 feet below the surface. In most places a sufficient supply of water for common needs seeps into the well from the lower part of the upper till or is furnished by springs found in thin seams of sand or gravel next below this, or within 15 or 20 feet in the lower till. The water in these wells usually rises slowly, allowing plenty of time for walling them; or often it is under no pressure, and a reservoir must be dug below its source. The experience of well-diggers frequently demonstrates that veins of gravel and sand filled with water under pressure may be quite narrow. Thus of several wells near together one only will encounter the vein, though the others go much deeper. The upward pressure and abundant supply of water, however, show that though narrow the vein is continuous through a considerable distance and descends from a higher level. It is probable that many of these courses of gravel and sand were formed by small sub-glacial streams.

Stratified beds of gravel, sand or clay were found between the upper and lower till, or lay beneath the upper till and were not passed through, in 127 wells; 77 of which showed 2 feet or less of this modified drift; 22 had between 2 and 10 feet; 7 between 10 and 20; and 21 had from 20 to 70 feet. The thickest of these beds were seldom penetrated. The west range of townships in Otter Tail county may be mentioned as a tract in which such large deposits of modified drift are frequently found under a comparatively thin surface of upper till.

Massive deposits of stratified gravel and sand in or beneath the lower till were found in 43 wells. The lower till above the modified drift in these wells averages 26 feet thick, its extremes being 5 and 53 feet. The underlying gravel and sand, with layers of clay in some instances, average 17 feet, and range from 5 to 70 feet in thickness.

Interglacial epochs, in which animals and plants lived upon this area, are proved by their remains preserved, evidently where they were living, in stratified beds underlain and overlain by till. Such fossiliferous beds, however, are very rarely found in this region, and the following enumeration includes all that have come to our knowledge. In sec. 30, Blakely, Scott county, W. R. Salisbury's well was yellow till, 15 feet; blue till, 30 feet; and "mud, like a lake bottom," three feet, this lowest bed containing many shells, grass, and apparently grains of wild rice. In Hutchinson, 5 miles east of the village, the well at Nancy Nutt's, in S. E. ¼ of sec. 35, was upper till, 14 feet; much harder lower till, 16 feet; and gray sand, 2 feet, the last containing abundant snail-shells, like those now living in our lakes. S. D. Ross' well, ¼ mile east of this, was similar, finding at the bottom a bed of sand filled with these shells. At Olivia station, in sec. 7, Bird Island, Renville county, the well at Lincoln Brothers' mill was yellow till, picked, 10 feet; softer but more rocky blue till, 9 feet; very hard blue till, 1 foot; and quicksand, 4 feet. A log, apparently tamarack, 8 inches in diameter, with several smaller sticks and twigs, lay across this well, embedded in the top of the quicksand. They were chopped off at each side. G. W. Burch, 2 miles south-west from this, in sec. 24, Troy, found upper till, 18 feet; dry, yellow sand, 4 feet; soft blue till, 15 feet; black loam, perhaps an interglacial soil, 2 feet; and gray quicksand, 4 feet, its upper part containing a log and smaller sticks like the foregoing. Several other wells within one or two miles about Olivia show similar remains of a deeply buried tamarack swamp. At Barnesville, in Clay county, John Marth's well was till, 12 feet; then, quicksand, 1 foot, containing several sticks of tamarack up to 8 inches in diameter, lying across the well, which, together with the inflow of water, prevented farther digging. In the N. E. ¼ of sec. 28, t. 135, r. 47, Wilkin county, C. R. Gleason's well was upper till, 8 feet; gray sand, ½ inch; much harder lower till, 18 feet; underlain by sandy black mud, containing many snail-shells. The two last are within the area that was afterward covered by Lake Agassiz. All these wells found a supply of water in the beds containing the fossils and therefore stopped before reaching the till which almost certainly underlies them. The locality first mentioned, in Blakely, is just at the top of the bluffs of Minnesota river, so that the entire depth of the drift at this place, composed about wholly of till, is known to be more than three times that of the well. The drift is probably of equal thickness in the other places; and, as shown by numerous wells 125 to 265 feet deep, it is generally composed of till, enclosing occasional stratified beds. Two other instances in which shells were found by wells in till, at Stewart and near Campbell, but where nothing definite has yet been learned about them; shells found in the brick clay at Chaska overlain by till; and a tamarack swamp at Fergus Falls, buried under 12 feet of very coarse fluvial deposits, complete this list. Though these examples are few in number, they yet are regarded as undeniable evidence that animals and plants occupied the land during temperate interglacial epochs, preceded and followed by an arctic climate and ice-sheets like those now covering the interior of Greenland and the Antarctic continent. The occurrence of interglacial shells and trees in the Red river valley appears to prove that the departure of the ice in their epoch was sufficient to allow the drainage of this valley northward.

If successive ice-sheets have thus been accumulated and pushed forward upon this area, some of them doubtless formed terminal moraines, which were afterward covered and their mounds and hills of coarsely rocky drift spread in a nearly level stratum by the more extended ice-sheet of a later epoch. Such a buried moraine is exposed by the deep channel of the upper Minnesota river. The till here is found to contain, at a depth of 40 or 50 feet below the general surface, a stratum that abounds in boulders, usually producing a narrow shelf or terrace upon the bluffs. About Correll station, in Big Stone county, this rocky layer in the till has caused an extensive plain to be left in the process of erosion, 50 feet below the top of the bluffs and about 75 feet above the river. It is everywhere plentifully strown with boulders, and in some portions these occur in heaps and patches covering half the ground. The deserted channels north-east of Lac qui Parle frequently have their bed upon this stratum of boulders. Its exposures along the Minnesota valley were seen in many places through a distance of 50 miles, extending from the Correll plain to a point three miles below the mouth of the Yellow Medicine river.

Modified Drift. In addition to the beds of modified drift enclosed in the till or lying below it, other accumulations deposited by water occur on the surface of areas which are mainly till. They consist of interstratified gravel and sand in knolls or mounds that rise 10 to 20 feet above the general level. These are seldom very numerous, and are rarely extended in ridges or in any noticeable series. Their origin, however, was probably similar to that of the gravel ridges or kames which often form long series in other drift regions, being the deposits of glacial rivers poured down from the surface of the melting ice-fields. The only place where kames of the usual type have been observed, occurring as well-marked parallel ridges of interbedded gravel and sand, is two miles south-east of Lake Johanna in Pope county. Here they are from 25 to 75 feet high, extending two miles from north to south, and the land at each side is modified drift. A less typical ridge of this kind forms the west shore of Wall lake, five miles east of Fergus Falls.

The lake deposits of the Red River valley have been partially described, and their origin treated of, in an earlier part of this report. A section of these beds at Glyndon, shown by a boring at the elevator of G. S. Barnes & Co., was soil, 3 feet; quicksand, 22 feet; dark clay, free from stones, 75 feet; very hard yellowish till, 15 feet; softer till, 10 feet. In Moorhead the well at John Erickson's brewery was light-colored clay, 20 feet; quicksand, 4 feet; blue clay, with gravel and boulders, 80 feet; underlain by sand from which water rose immediately about 80 feet. A. H. Moore's well at Fargo, within a mile west from the last, was similar, being yellow clay, 15 feet; sand, 3 feet; dark, bluish clay, 77 feet, free from pebbles, excepting in its last two feet; underlain by sand from which water rose to 7 feet below the surface. At Georgetown, 16 miles north from these, a well 80 feet deep was wholly in stratified clay, yellowish for about 10 feet at the top and dark bluish below, finding no sandy layers and no water.

The modified drift which covers the greater part of eastern Becker and Otter Tail counties is in contrast with this plain of lacustrine clay, being almost wholly sand and fine gravel, sometimes level, again moderately undulating,

4

and occasionally, as at Detroit, in swells and hills 25 to 40 feet high. These deposits are not often penetrated by wells, which show them to be in some places at least 80 feet deep. Southward, similar accumulations of sand and gravel are found in the east edge of Douglas and Pope counties, while eastward they have a large extent outside the limits of this report. They are believed to have been deposited by descending floods produced and freighted by a departing ice-sheet, which appears to have sloped toward this area from the west, north, and east.

Glacial melting also filled the great valleys with stratified gravel, sand and clay. Clearwater and Monticello prairies in Wright county are expansions of this glacial flood-plain of the Mississippi. Since the ice-age the river has channelled out and carried away much of these deposits, leaving remnants upon each side. At Monticello and Clearwater these plains of modified drift are 70 to 80 feet above the river. Between them and the bottomland, or flood-plain of the present time, an intermediate terrace is frequently seen. Monticello village is situated on such an area, about 35 feet above the river. Northward, at St. Cloud and Brainerd, the old flood-plain is about 60 feet high; to the southeast it descends a little faster than the river, its height being 45 feet at Dayton, and from 25 to 30 at the head of St. Anthony's falls.

The valley of the Minnesota river from Mankato to its mouth was also filled with modified drift. Its remnants include a terrace 3 miles long east and south of Kasota; the "sand prairie" about 4 miles long and averaging a mile wide, west and north of St. Peter; Le Sueur prairie, 6 miles long and from 1 to 3 miles wide, beginning east of Ottawa and reaching to Le Sueur; the plain 5 miles long and a mile wide, near the middle of which Belle Plaine is built; Spirit hill and "sand prairie," south-west and north-west of Jordan; a terrace 8 miles long and varying from a few rods to 2 miles in width, extending through San Francisco, Dahlgren, and Carver; and Shakopee prairie, 8 miles long and averaging one mile wide. The height of these plains at Kasota, St. Peter, and Le Sueur, is about 150 feet above the river; at Belle Plaine, about 135; and at Jordan, Carver, and Shakopee, about 125. Wells on the "sand prairie" near St. Peter and on Le Sueur prairie go through sand and gravel, sometimes with layers of clay, to the depth of 75 or 100 feet, finding till below. At Belle Plaine the sand and gravel are about 50 feet deep, underlain by till. Shakopee prairie has 40 or 50 feet of this modified drift, lying upon limestone. The principal remnant of these deposits seen below Shakopee was a terrace about 75 feet high, $\frac{1}{8}$ to $\frac{1}{3}$ mile wide, and 4 miles long, extending through Eagan in Dakota county, its north end being about 2 miles south of Fort Snelling. This valley was first excavated in till, which rises in continuous bluffs on each side 50 to 100 feet above these high plains and terraces of modified drift. It was afterward filled for 60 miles next to its mouth with fluvial deposits 75 to 150 feet thick, sloping about 2 feet per mile, through which the channel has been cut anew. Above Mankato the valley rarely shows any similar remnants of modified drift; and those which are found appear to have been part of local accumulations, rather than of a continuous flood-plain. Further remarks relating to the orgin of the modified drift in this valley are to be found in the description, under the ensuing division of this report, of the brick clays at Chaska, Carver, and Jordan.

51

The chief contributions to the wealth of Minnesota, derived directly from geological formations in this district, are bricks, lime, and quarried stone. Explorations made for coal, its mode of occurrence, and the improbability that it exists here in any valuable amount, have been spoken of in our account of the cretaceous strata. No ores of any practical importance have been found. The principal resources of this part of the State are the products of its invariably fertile soil, and the water-powers afforded by many of its streams, which, by using their lakes for reservoirs, may be made nearly uniform in flow throughout the year.

Bricks. Notes respecting the manufacture of bricks have been gathered wherever this work is done, and part of these are here presented. The material employed is usually stratified clay, belonging to the modified drift; sometimes along Minnesota River it is the alluvium now being deposited at every season of high water; and rarely, as at Fergus Falls, the clay used in brick-making appears to be a true till, in which portions quite free from gravel can be selected. The bricks made from the recent alluvial clay are red, but nearly all others throughout this region are cream-colored, this difference being due to the state of chemical combination assumed during the process of burning by the iron which these clays contain.

The following statements show the extent of this industry in the Valley of Minnesota River, where bricks are made at many places, among which Chaska leads with a yearly product of about seven millions. The order is that found in ascending the river.

At Shakopee, Schrœder Brothers have made bricks 4 years; annual product, 700,000, selling at $5 per M. Alluvial clay is used, with admixture of one part sand to two of clay.

At Chaska four companies are engaged in this business, all upon an area about an eighth of a mile in extent. This clay is modified drift of interglacial age. It varies from 20 to 40 feet in thickness, being underlain by sand and covered by till from 2 to 6 feet thick, holding boulders of all sizes up to 5 or 6 feet in diameter, many of which are planed and striated. This till forms the surface, 25 to 30 feet above the river. The only fossils found here were fresh-water mussel shells, which occurred in considerable numbers upon a space four rods in diameter near the middle of Gregg & Griswold's excavation, lying in the upper foot of the clay, just beneath the till. Brick-making was begun here twelve years ago, and has been steadily increasing to the present time. The first yard worked has been now owned by Gregg & Griswold six years. Their yearly product is about 2500 thousand, selling at $5 to $6 per M. From 40 to 50 men are employed for six months. Sand is mixed in varying proportions according to the quality of the clay, the average being about one part in ten. This company have machinery and room to make 40 thousand bricks daily. L. Warner makes about two millions yearly, employing 30 men. The proportion of sand used is from one-fourth to one-seventh. Wiest & Kruze make 1500 thousand yearly, having 20 men. The two last yards have been operated about 8 years. Schlafle, Strobach & Streissguth began three years ago, and in 1878 made 900 thousand; during 1879, they expected to make three millions, employing 40 men.

At Carver the clay used occurs 50 to 90 feet above the river, as a stratum from 30 to 40 feet thick, overlain and underlain by sand, being included in the modified drift which formerly filled this part of the valley. It probably was deposited during the retreat of the ice-sheet which overspread this region, as shown by the interglacial clay at Chaska, after the valley had been excavated between its bluffs of till. J. M. Nye & Co. here make 300 to 500 thousand bricks yearly; and Andrew Ahlin, about two-thirds of a mile southwest from Carver, has two yards, his annual product being from one to one and a half millions.

At Jordan Charles Rodell has made bricks 12 years, averaging about 500 thousand yearly, and selling at $6 per M. This clay deposit, as at Carver, is part of the stratified valley drift. It is 40 feet thick, lying upon till, and overlain by gravel and sand. The top of the clay is about 65 feet above the river. A very interesting kind of stratification is shown by this clay, which is bedded in distinct horizontal layers from 3 to 8 inches thick, averaging 6 inches. These layers are dark bluish, often finely laminated, changing above and below to a nearly black, more unctuous and finer clay, which forms the partings between them. These divisions are clearly seen through the whole extent of Mr. Rodell's excavation, which reaches 25 feet below the top of the clay and is 4 rods long. The same stratification is shown also by the excavation of Nye & Co. at Carver, where the exposure is 4 rods long and 15 feet high, except that here the layers all have a nearly uniform thickness of 3 inches. In this depth of 15 feet there are thus about sixty layers, all exactly alike. The alternating conditions which produced them were evidently repeated sixty times in uninterrupted succession. The only explanation for this which seems possible is that these divisions mark so many years occupied by the deposition of this clay. It appears that these clay-beds are of limited extent. The broad flood-plain was mainly built up by additions of fine gravel and sand spread over its surface by floods like those which now occasionally overflow the bottom-lands. Clay could settle only where hollows were formed by inequalities in this deposition and left outside the path of the principal current. Now nearly all the features of the modified drift, as the general absence of shells or other fossils, its hillocks and ridges called kames, and its occurrence only in glaciated regions or in valleys of drainage from them, indicate that this formation was accumulated by streams discharged from a melting ice-sheet. If the origin of the modified drift that filled the lower part of the Minnesota Valley was from such glacial melting, it is apparent that the floods would be greater and would bring and deposit more sediment in summer than in winter. Layers nearly like those in the clay at Carver and Jordan are also seen in other clay-beds in this valley and in that of the Mississippi in this State. The principal mass of each layer is regarded as the deposition during the warm portion of a year, and the very dark partings as the sediment during winter when the melting was less and the water consequently less turbid. The upper part of these beds of clay are generally colored yellow to a depth varying from one or two to ten feet, the lower portion being blue. The limit of the yellow color in the clay at Jordan runs obliquely, being nearly parallel with the sloping surface, so that the same horizontal layers are partly blue and partly yellow, which shows that this is a discoloration by weathering.

At Belle Plaine, Jacob Kranz has made bricks 10 years; annual product,

300 thousand, selling at $5 to $6 per M. The clay used is recent alluvium of the river, with which he mixes one-sixth as much sand as clay.

At Henderson bricks are made by Herman Matthei, who began 9 years ago, and now averages 400 thousand yearly ; and by John Meier, who began in 1878, and expected to make 300 thousand during last season. Both use recent alluvium.

At LeSueur Henry Kruze has made bricks 16 years, using alluvial clay; annual product, 300 thousand. He mixes one part of sand with two of clay. J. Wetter also has made bricks here 8 years, averaging 100 thousand per year. His clay has a thickness of 5 feet, and is underlain by sand, the two forming a terrace about 100 feet above the river.

In Oshawa, about one mile south-west from St. Peter, Matthias Davidson has made bricks 19 years, using the recent alluvium. He averages 400 thousand yearly, and sells at $4 to $7 per M.

The brick-making at Mankato and New Ulm cannot be here reported. At Redwood Falls two kilns of brick, about 200 thousand, were burned by Bohn & Lamberton in 1878. The clay is about 40 feet above the top of the succession of falls here in Redwood river, and about 180 feet above Minnesota river. The section is black soil, 2 feet; yellow clay, dipping slightly eastward, about 7 feet; changing below to yellowish sand. This clay is in layers, mostly about 8 inches thick, divided by dark partings similar to those described at Carver and Jordan. The underlying sand is in layers from $\frac{1}{4}$ to 1 inch thick, separated by hard films of iron-rust. Attempts to make bricks at Minnesota Falls and Granite Falls have failed, because of small limy concretions in the clay, causing them to crack in burning. Bricks in this region command $8 per M.

At Montevideo, Nils Swennungson has made bricks two years; annual product, 60 thousand, selling at $6 to $10 per M. This clay is on the general level of the upland, 100 feet above the river. The section is soil, $1\frac{1}{2}$ feet ; yellow clay, used for brick-making, 3 feet ; clayey sand, 6 inches ; with clay containing limy concretions below.

At Big Stone City in Dakota, opposite Ortonville, Tobias Oehler began brick-making this year (1879). The clay is nearly like that of Montevideo. During this season he made 240 thousand, selling at $12 per M.

Brief notes of this production in counties north of the Minnesota river are the following, arranged in their order from south-east to north-west : $\frac{1}{2}$ mile west of Dayton, in Otsego, Wright county, by Medor Arseno, about 250 M. yearly, at $7 to $8 per M.; at Cokato, Wright county, by James Runions, 300 M. yearly, for six years, at $8, the clay now nearly exhausted ; 2 miles north of Hutchinson, McLeod county, by W. H. Wyman, 100 M. yearly, at $7 to $8 ; 3 miles north-east from Litchfield, Meeker county, by Henry Ames, 500 M. yearly at $7; at the north-west side of Nest lake in New London, Kandiyohi county, by Peter Larson, Jr., 200 to 300 M. yearly, at $8 to $10 ; at DeGraff, Swift county, 300 M. were made in 1877, selling at $10 per M.; at Glenwood, Pope county, by John Aiton, 150 to 300 M. yearly, at $7 to $10 ; $1\frac{1}{2}$ miles north-east of Alexandria, Douglas county, by John A. McKay, 500 M. yearly, at $6 to $10 ; 3 miles south-west of Alexandria, in sec. 2, Lake Mary township, by Mark Bundy, 75 M. yearly ; $\frac{1}{2}$ mile north-west of Evansville station, Douglas county, by Richard Partridge, about 40 M. yearly at $10 ; about 3 miles west of Parker's Prairie, Otter Tail county, by Henry Asseln, 100 M. in 1878, at $7 to $10; at Fergus Falls, by J. A. Nelson & Brothers, 100 M. formerly, 600 M. this year (1879), at about $8; 3 miles west of Fergus Falls, by S. R. Childs, 150 M. this year; at Detroit, Becker county, by Shaw & Martin, about 200 M. yearly at $8; and at Moorhead, by Lamb Brothers, 2500 M. yearly, at $6, and by Kruegel & Truitt, 1200 M. yearly. Additional details respecting this work and these and other deposits of clay adapted for brick-making, will be given in the final report.

Lime. The abundance or frequent occurrence of boulders and pebbles of magnesian limestone in the drift of this entire district, has been mentioned in describing that formation. The same stone, more finely pulverized, is one of the most important ingredients of our sand and clay also, being a principal cause of the great fertility of the soil throughout all these counties. A large part of the lime used for building, except along or near the lower Minnesota river, has been derived from the drift, its limestone boulders being gathered upon rocky, morainic areas, or about shallow lakes, where the expansion of the ice in winters has slowly pushed these and other rock-fragments outward to the shore. A little ridge of gravel and boulders is thus frequently heaped to a height varying from four to eight feet above the lake. In nearly every county several of the early settlers have availed themselves of this resource, constructing small kilns and burning from 50 to 200 barrels of lime yearly, according to the demand in their vicinity. This lime is usually of excellent quality, contains little sand, and is white, or sometimes cream-colored. We have a large list of these lime-burners, but can mention here only those who do a permanent and considerable business, as follow: at Dayton, Levi Guier, burning about 500 barrels of lime yearly, sold at $1 per barrel; in Greenleaf, Meeker county, Lewis Maher, from 100 to 300 barrels yearly, at $1.50; near Beaver Falls, Renville county, John Edget, R. R. Corey, and several others, each about 100 barrels yearly, at $1.50; at Minnesota Falls, Simon Christianson and W. C. Darby, each 300 barrels yearly, at $1.50; one mile north of Ortonville, Alfred Knowlton, 500 barrels this year at $1.25; farther north-west, beside Big Stone lake, Jacob Hurley, E. T. Hanes, and William H. Bowman, selling yearly from 150 to 300 barrels each, at $1.25; at Donnelly, Stevens county, Joseph Meier, 300 to 400 barrels yearly, at $1.25; in Evansville, Douglas county, Partridge Brothers, 250 barrels yearly, at $1.25; in Leaf Mountain and Clitherall, Otter Tail county, Orris Albertson and others, 200 barrels or more yearly, at $1.25; at Fergus Falls, J. A. Nelson & Brothers, and E. Barbeau, each about 500 barrels yearly, at $1; in south part of Oscar, Otter Tail county, Peter Carlson, about 400 barrels yearly, at $1; in Eglon, Clay county, Nils Larson, from 75 to 250 barrels yearly, at $1; and at Detroit and White Earth Agency, Becker county, Shaw& Martin, 500 barrels yearly, at $1.50.

Limestone in fragments and pulverized is so large an ingredient of the drift that all percolating waters become more or less charged with carbonate of lime in solution. The soft rain-water is thus changed to hard water before it finds its way into wells or issues in springs. The limestone which the water has taken up forms a scale on the inside of tea-kettles and the boilers of engines; and similarly, because of exposure to the open air and evaporation, it is occasionally deposited by springs as an incrustation of moss, leaves, or other objects, or as a porous bed upon the surface of springy ground. Interesting springs of this kind occur near Carver, Glenwood, and Big Stone City. Their calcareous deposit is commonly called "petrified moss," from the fact that it becomes covered with growing moss, the lower part of which is being slowly encrusted and its form preserved by this accumulation. It is usually a light gray, very porous mass, less than a foot thick, and mixed with earth and foreign matter; but in two places more massive deposits of this origin are found, which appear to have a value for the manufacture of lime. One of these, occurring in the N. E. ¼ of sec 26 and south part of sec. 23, Tunsburg, Chippewa county, has been considerably burned for lime by E. R. Harkness, who states that it yields a nearly pure, white lime, fully as strong as that of boulders. It here forms a nearly level layer 2 to 3 feet thick, extending fully a half mile as shown by frequent exposures upon the side of the bluff of till north-east of the Chippewa river. Only its south-east portion is adapted for lime-burning, the rest being gravelly. It appears to mark a line at which springs issued because of impervious beds above or below it. These springs are now partly intercepted by a tributary ravine 30 rods north-east, in which "petrified moss" is forming along a distance of about an eighth of a mile, at a height of three to six feet above the rill. About twenty-five miles south-east from this, in the N. W. ¼ of section 22, south township of Hawk Creek, Renville county, a nearly compact calcareous deposit, containing impressions of leaves and sticks, is exposed for six to eight feet vertically in two masses four rods apart, on the south side of a ravine about fifty feet deep. It was probably formed by springs when this ravine was first channelled out, shortly after the glacial period.

Cretaceous strata in the vicinity of New Ulm, and the Shakopee limstone in the lower Minnesota valley, yield the most important supplies of lime derived from this district. The only kiln burning Cretaceous limestone north of Minnesota river and therefore within the limit of this district, is John Heymann's, about a half mile north of Redstone. His yearly product is from 1,000 to 1,500 barrels, sold at $1 per barrel. The section is soil, 2 feet; drift gravel, 1½ feet; cavernous, nodular, gray limestone, 2 feet; green clay with layers of red, 2 feet; and limestone as above, 2 feet; said to be underlain by clays and shales. These beds form a terrace about 35 feet above the river. Other kilns burning lime from this formation are situated on the opposite side of the river. This lime is strong and sets quickly, making a white plaster; except that it commonly includes a little clay, it is quite pure, having no magnesia or sand.

The Shakopee limestone gives a very dark lime, which slacks to a brown or cream color. It is magnesian, with a little admixture of sand, and is burned more easily, slacks with less heat, and sets more slowly, than pure lime. It is preferred by masons for brick and stone work, and for plastering except the finishing coat. The following notes were gathered respecting the manufacture of lime from this formation. At Shakopee, J. B. Conter burns 15,000 barrels yearly, selling it at Saint Paul and Minneapolis for 55 cents per barrel of 200 pounds. The section here is limestone, obscurely and irregularly bedded, yielding leather-colored lime, 6 to 8 feet; a lighter-colored calcareous sandstone, divided in beds about 8 inches thick, somewhat used for building stone, 2 feet; limestone nearly as above, in irregular beds from a few inches to one foot thick, yielding a very dark, blackish lime, 12 feet.

The stratification is nearly level; but all the beds are more or less fractured, porous and cavernous, with different colors in the same layer a rod apart. The color throughout is buff of various shades approaching pink, yellow, and brown. The top of the quarry is about 50 feet above the river, and this formation extends below to the water's edge. Mr. Conter also burns about 15,000 barrels of lime yearly at a quarry 5 miles to the south-west in Louisville. This limestone is nearly like that at Shakopee. It is arenaceous, but shows no continuous layer of sandstone. At Ottawa, Charles Schwartz burns about 400 barrels of lime yearly for the demand in his vicinity, selling at 60 cents per barrel. At Caroline, in sec. 17, Kasota, Conrad Smith burns 6,000 barrels yearly, selling at 55 cents per barrel. A third of a mile southeast from the last, George C. Clapp has burned lime 20 years, averaging 2,000 barrels yearly, but has done nothing in this business during the last two years. The last three use only the upper 2 to 5 feet of the limestone terrace at these places. A large amount of lime is also burned from the Shakopee limestone in Mankato, which is not included in this report.

The St. Lawrence limestone in sec. 13, Jessenland, Sibley county, has been used for lime-burning by Herman Matthei, brick-maker at Henderson. Five kilns of small size were burned here last year, but the stone is now teamed to Henderson before burning. The lime brings 60 cents per barrel.

Quarried Stone. The formations which are quarried in the valley of Minnesota river for building stone, foundations, bridge masonry, or similar uses, are the quartzyte at Redstone, and the three members of the Lower Magnesian group. The granite and gneiss of the upper Minnesota valley have not yet been worked to any considerable extent, but will probably furnish valuable quarries for the general market when a demand is created by the more complete settlement and increasing wealth of that region. Cretaceous sandstone, as previously mentioned, has been quarried slightly for culverts and cellar-walls in Courtland, 8 and 11 miles south-east from New Ulm; but the business is now discontinued or very small.

In the quartzyte at Redstone quarries are owned by Francis Baasen, about 30 rods south-east from the railroad-bridge, who formerly quarried $200 worth of stone yearly, but none for three years past; William Winkelmann, a few rods farther east, quarrying only for his own use in building; Frederick Meierding, a little farther east, now selling $100 worth yearly, formerly about $400 yearly; Gottlieb Arndt, one-fifth mile north-east from last, with annual sales from $50 to $300; and Joseph Reinhart, close east of the last, selling little now, formerly $300 worth per year. Only rough stone of small dimension is obtained, bringing from $2 to $3 per cord.

Quarries in the limestone at St. Lawrence are owned by Abraham Bisson and Philip Corbel, both renting to others the privilege to quarry for 50 cents a cord. The stone is sold at $3 or $3.50 per cord, the first of these quarries supplying fifty cords yearly and the second about twenty cords yearly. The sales for stone work from the quarries in Faxon and Jessenland are still smaller. Of this limestone at Hebron, in the south part of Nicollet township, quarries are owned, in order from east to west, by Abel Keene, William J. Phillips, William H. Thurston, and Mrs. J. H. Dunham. Some of these are rented at 50 cents per cord. The stone is sold for $3 per cord, and the extent of sales at each quarry varies from $100 to $300 yearly. Judson, opposite to Hebron, has other small quarries in this formation.

The Jordan sandstone is quarried at Jordan by Frank Nicolin and Philip Kipp. It lies in beds from eight inches to two or three feet thick. Mr. Nicolin's flour-mill at this place, built of this stone, is 60 by 70 feet in area and 75 feet high, in six stories, having its walls 5 feet thick at the base and 20 inches at the top. Besides this structure, which was erected in 1878 and 1879, Mr. Nicolin's quarry has within three years supplied $2000 worth of stone, sold to the Minneapolis & St. Louis railroad for bridge masonry and to other purchasers. Mr. Kipp's quarry, opened this year, has supplied about $200 worth, at $3.75 per cord. Foss, Wells & Co. also quarried this stone to build their mill and elevator.

The limestone at Shakopee is too much seamed and fractured and too irregularly bedded for use as a building stone. In ascending the river, quarries where stone is obtained from this formation for building purposes are found in Louisville, Ottawa, St. Peter, Kasota, and Mankato, the two last places having the largest business. This work at Mankato we cannot report. Opposite to this city, in Belgrade, three quarries on the land of John Q. A. Marsh and brother are rented mostly to Dennis Sullivan and John Duffee, who pay 50 cents per cord, selling at about $2 per cord for rough stone. A little further west, Andrew M. Wiemar owns a quarry opened last year. He supplies dimension stone, rough or hammered. The rock of these quarries is evenly colored and compact, in thick beds, and can supply blocks 5 by 4 by 2 feet, or slabs 8 feet long. Details of the other places are given in the order mentioned.

In Louisville, Mrs. M. A. Spencer owns a quarry which has been worked 15 years, with annual sales from $200 to $950. This stone is in layers from 1 to 3 feet thick, hard and compact, except that small cavities sometimes occur in it. It has been used for much of the bridge masonry of Scott and Carver counties, including the railroad-bridges at Chaska and Carver.

At Ottawa quarries are owned by Levi Case, John R. Clark, Robert Todd, John S. Randall, Robert Winegar, and Kasper Mäder. The annual product is from 50 to 300 cords from each, sold at $1 to $2.50 per cord. The stone here is in layers from a few inches to one foot thick. It is sold mostly for use within 10 or 15 miles to wall cellars and wells, little being sent away on the cars.

At St. Peter the stone is thinly bedded as at Ottawa, except in the Asylum quarry, where it lies in massive beds 1 to 4 feet thick. This quarry has been worked principally for the Asylum buildings. The other quarries are owned or worked by Jacob Bauer, Hugh Brogan, Ubalt Drenttel, John Malgren, and Henry Miller. Their annual product is 50 to 200 cords each, selling at $1.50 to $3 per cord.

Kasota has the best quarries found in this limestone within our limits. It is in beds from 6 inches to 2½ feet thick, pinkish buff in color, uniform in its texture, easily cut into any desired form, and durable under exposure to the weather. The most extensive business here is that of Breen & Young, who lease from Stewart, Breckenridge & Butters. They employ 35 men and 3 teams at quarrying and loading upon the cars, the product in 1879 being worth $15,000 as rough stone; it is dressed after reaching their shops in Saint Paul and Minneapolis, which brings their sales per year to about $30,000. The largest stone ever shipped by them weighed 10 tons, its dimensions in feet being 14 by 8 by 1. Their quarry can supply blocks of large size and 2 or 2½ feet thick; slabs, as for cemetery borders, 20 feet long; and flag-stones 10 or 12 feet square and eight inches thick. Examples of the stone from this quarry are the residence of H. J. Willing, of the firm of Field, Leiter & Co., in Chicago; the First Baptist Church in Saint Paul; trimmings of the High School Building in Minneapolis; and trimmings of the State Prison in Stillwater. The only other quarry at this place is owned by J. W. Babcock, whose yearly sales are from $5,000 to $10,000. He has used stone to cut up which formed an unbroken sheet 60 feet long. Examples from this quarry are the trimmings of Odd Fellows' Hall in Saint Paul, and of Plymouth Church in Minneapolis.

www.ingramcontent.com/pod-product-compliance
Lightning Source LLC
Chambersburg PA
CBHW031754090426
42739CB00008B/1008